Whispers to the Soul

Orange Books Publication

1st Floor, Rajhans Arcade, Mall Road, Kohka, Bhilai, Chhattisgarh 490020
Website: **www.orangebooks.in**

First Edition, 2025

ISBN: 978-93-6554-746-7

Price: Rs. 396.00

Printed in India

WHISPERS TO THE SOUL

DAILY AFFIRMATIONS FOR A LIFE REIMAGINED

SHILPY TANDON

Orange Books Publication
www.orangebooks.in

A heartfelt thank you to **Ms Drishti Arya (📷 Instagram: @drishtiaryaphotography)** *for generously allowing us to use her stunning photograph as the inspiration for the cover page of my Journal, "Whispers to the Soul: Daily Affirmations for a life Reimagined." Your talent and artistry have truly brought this vision to life, and we are deeply grateful for your contribution to this journey. Your work has inspired and added a soulful touch to this creation. Thank you for sharing your gift with us!*

Dedication

This journal is lovingly dedicated to my beloved **father**, whose absence still echoes in every quiet moment of my journey. His blessings continue to guide me, silently but strongly, like the roots beneath a tree, unseen, yet essential. His encouragement was never loud, but it was constant, kind, and unwavering. Even now, I feel his presence as a warm breeze in moments of doubt and a calm anchor in storms of uncertainty.

To **Mr S S Nair**, my dear friend, whose fierce support and heartfelt belief became the torchlight in the darkest moments of this creation. Your presence has been nothing short of divine timing, a reminder that true friendship strengthens dreams when they are still fragile.

To the family's beloved children, **Nirosha, Rhythm**, and **Simran**, whose light, innocence, and laughter illuminate every dream I pursue. You are the living symbols of hope, joy, and endless possibilities, the future for whom every seed of love, strength, and wisdom is tenderly sown.

To my mother, **Mrs Nirmal Tandon**, whose prayers, sacrifices, and quiet resilience are the true foundation of every step I take. Your unwavering faith in me has been my shelter, my courage, and my silent anthem.

This book is the result of both visible and invisible hands, those who lift, love, and lead without needing recognition. It is a testament to bonds that transcend words, to love that empowers silently, and to blessings that never leave, even when the eyes cannot see them.

Author's Note

Dear Reader,

This journal wasn't simply written, it was lived. Every affirmation, every reflection, and every chapter carries pieces of my journey: the tears, the triumphs, the deep breaths, and the unwavering belief that healing is always possible. Growing up, I never fit into the box's others placed me in. I struggled with my weight through school and college, often mocked and underestimated. But with faith, focus, and the power of manifestation, I transformed not just my body but my purpose. For the past 19 years, I've walked alongside hundreds of people, helping them rewrite their fitness stories with compassion and realism.

Yet, that was just one part of my transformation. I have dyslexia, a challenge that made reading and writing a struggle for most of my life. The idea of authoring a book once felt like a far-off dream, even laughable to some. Friends still help me correct my spelling. But I've learned that you don't wait to be perfect to begin, you begin, even if it's messy, because your voice matters.

This book is proof that limits exist only in the mind. It is a quiet space for reflection. A mirror for your soul. A sacred companion you can return to whenever the world feels too loud. I created it for anyone who's ever been told they couldn't, so they remember they always can. So, speak these affirmations out loud. Breathe with intention. Come back here as often as you need. You are not alone.

❀ ***"True health begins in the mind, blossoms in the body, and lives in the spirit."***

With all my love,

- Shilpy Tandon

Acknowledgements

I would like to express my deepest gratitude to every soul who touched this journey with love, light, and encouragement. To my dearest friends and family, your timely support, thoughtful presence, and gentle nudges brought this dream into the light. Your belief in me made this book possible.

To all my mentors and well-wishers who unknowingly guided me through their words, blessings, and wisdom, thank you for being anchors when I felt unsteady.

To **Jai Guru Ji**, whose divine grace, spiritual protection, and infinite light held me steady through every chapter of this manifestation. This book is not just my work, it is your blessing channelled through me and to the readers who will hold this journal in their hands. Thank you for trusting me with your heart.

About the Author

Ms Shilpy Tandon is more than an author; she is a living embodiment of the transformational power of manifestation, mindfulness, and inner alignment. With roots grounded in discipline, compassion, and a visionary mindset, Shilpy has journeyed from self-discovery to global impact, bringing together the worlds of fitness, emotional well-being, and spiritual awareness into one meaningful path.

A certified Advanced ***Yoga*** Therapist from the revered *Shivananda Ashram,* Shilpy blends ancient wisdom with modern tools, empowering people across borders to connect with their inner strength. With deep expertise and certified in ***TRX, Fitness Testing, Prenatal, Postnatal, Aerobics, Step Aerobics, Weight loss, Personal Training, Nutrition, Taping, Reiki and holistic health***, she designs personalised wellness programs that go far beyond the physical, addressing the body, mind, and soul as one unified whole.

Through the conscious practice of manifestation, mindfulness, and goal perspective clarity, Shilpy personally achieved a remarkable transformation, journeying from 84 kilograms to 58 kilograms, a living testament to the power of inner work, intention, and resilience. Her inspiring health journey has also been proudly featured in *Prevention Magazine*, showcasing her as an authentic example of self-driven change.

She is a motivator who believes success is not accidental; it is manifested. Her achievements are not just goals reached, but dreams lived, born from focus, faith, and fierce determination. From overcoming personal and professional challenges to organising community wellness programs and guiding international clients, her journey reflects what's possible when intention meets disciplined action.

With her experience and years of work in building decentralised, client-focused training modules, she brings a structured yet soulful approach to transformation. Her book on affirmations and life manifestations reflects her truth, rooted in real experience, shaped by the values of gratitude, family, and spiritual growth.

Email: shilpy.tandon@gmail.com

Instagram: @shilpytandon

How to Use This Journal

This journal is not meant to be rushed. Instead, treat each chapter as a meditation, an intentional pause to nourish your inner world. Here's how to use it:

1. **One Chapter at a Time:** Start with any topic calling to you.
2. **Read Slowly:** Absorb personal insight, visualisation, and affirmations.
3. **Use the Reflection Space:** After each chapter, journal your thoughts, emotions, and inspired actions.
4. **Return Often:** Revisit affirmations when you need to realign.
5. **Make It Yours:** Highlight, underline, draw, let your energy live on these pages.

Chapters 1–62 cover manifestations across various aspects of health, career, relationships, emotional healing, spirituality, and life goals.

Feel free to scan through the Table of Contents or flip to any page that calls your heart.

Each page is an invitation to remember that you are *always* manifesting. Consciously. Lovingly. Powerfully.

❀ "This journal began with a whisper. May it leave you with a roar of possibility."

Contents

Unfolding Gracefully: Reclaiming Your Inherent Worth

1. Manifesting the Desired Health with Peace of Mind

"Every cell in my body vibrates with health, vitality, and peace."

A Personal Insight

Health isn't just about what shows up on a medical report. It's how deeply you feel at ease in your body, how gently you speak to yourself, and how lovingly you treat your own energy. We've all been conditioned to think of health in terms of numbers, weight, or prescriptions, but real wellness is quiet, personal, and deeply rooted in inner peace.

Peace of mind is not a luxury. It's the soil where good health grows. When our thoughts are kind, when our sleep is restful, and when we move with intention, our bodies begin to respond. Healing doesn't always look dramatic; it often begins with soft, subtle changes.

A Moment to Visualise

Find a quiet spot. Breathe deeply, hold gently, and release. Now picture your body as a glowing field of light. Every part of you is alive, calm, and supported. Imagine yourself stretching, smiling, walking under the morning sun. See the tension melting away. Feel peace soaking into your bones.

Repeat Softly…. *"I welcome peace. I choose health. I allow my body to thrive."*

✵ Today's Affirmations

1. **"This body is where I live, and I choose to care for it gently, like a sacred space."**
2. **"There's harmony flowing through me, I can feel it in every heartbeat and breath."**
3. **"What I feel is not who I am. I hold space for healing and watch myself rise."**
4. **"I fill my plate with healing foods and fill my mind with calming thoughts."**
5. **"Stillness is strength. Calmness brings clarity. I let both guide my healing."**
6. **"Each breath leads me back to my centre, reminding me I belong to myself."**
7. **"It's okay to take time to rest. My worth isn't measured by how fast I move."**
8. **"My healing doesn't have to rush; it unfolds slowly, like the morning sun."**
9. **"My body knows the way back to balance, I'm here to support its journey."**
10. **"Today, I choose peace over pressure, care over control, and ease over effort."**

🌿 One Small Step

Take a moment today to drink water slowly; yes, just water. As it touches your lips, pause. With each sip, say quietly, **"Thank you, body. I see you. I support you."** This small act is a powerful beginning.

🙏 A Note to Close With

Each day offers a fresh chance to return to yourself. Write one thing your body allows you to do today, no matter how small and offer it your thanks.

"Healing isn't a destination. It's a soft, steady return to who you truly are."

📓 Your Reflection Space

……………………………………………………………………

……………………………………………………………………

……………………………………………………………………

……………………………………………………………………

2. Manifesting Abundance with an Open Heart

"Abundance is not something we acquire. It's something we tune into."

A Personal Insight

Abundance isn't just a number in a bank account or the luxury we see in glossy magazines. It's a quiet confidence, a sense of knowing that what you need will arrive, and that life flows generously when we stop resisting.

True abundance begins inside. It starts when we stop counting what's missing and begin appreciating what's already here. Every breath, every kind word, every opportunity to grow, these are signs that life is already in motion, working for you, not against you.

The heart that trusts becomes a magnet. When you shift your inner talk from "I lack" to "I welcome," you change your frequency. The world responds. Doors open. Ideas come. People show up. And slowly, you step into a space where abundance doesn't feel like a dream; it becomes your natural state of being.

🌈 A Moment to Visualise

Close your eyes. Imagine yourself standing under a gentle waterfall of golden light. This light carries the energy of ease, flow, and generosity. You feel it touching your heart, your hands, your thoughts. Picture yourself receiving what you've always hoped for: a peaceful home, financial freedom, and purposeful work.

See the joy on your face. Feel the calm in your chest. Let this moment remind you: you are ready to receive.

Repeat softly: "I am open to life's blessings. I receive with gratitude. I live in flow."

✨ Today's Affirmations

1. **"Abundance flows to me because I trust life to support me."**
2. **"Every day, I see new signs that I am richly provided for."**
3. **"I release fear around money and welcome prosperity with grace."**
4. **"The more I give with joy, the more I receive with ease."**
5. **"My worth is not defined by numbers; it's written in how I show up in the world."**
6. **"Opportunities find me because I am open and aligned."**
7. **"I celebrate other people's success; it shows me what's possible."**

8. **"Wealth to me means peace, purpose, and enough to share."**

9. **"I honour the flow of abundance by staying generous and grateful."**

10. **"Everything I need is already on its way to me."**

🌿 One Small Step

Take a coin, note, or token and place it in your palm. Hold it gently, close your eyes, and say: "This is energy. I let it move freely. I trust its return." Then, give it away. Buy someone a cup of tea, donate it, or tuck it into a note for someone to find. Watch how it feels to let go with love.

🙏 A Note to Close With

Abundance begins when we stop chasing and start aligning. Today, write down one small blessing you received that didn't cost money, but filled your heart. A smile. A peaceful moment. A kind word. These are seeds. They grow into so much more.

"Gratitude isn't just an emotion; it's the frequency that unlocks abundance."

📓 Your Reflection Space

....

....

....

....

3. Manifesting Weight Loss through Self-Respect and Joyful Movement

"I release the weight that no longer serves me, physical, emotional, and mental and return to my natural rhythm."

A Personal Insight

Weight loss is often spoken of in terms of numbers, diets, or routines. But beneath all that, it's a journey of *returning,* to your own body, your breath, your inner balance.

The true shift begins when we stop punishing ourselves and start listening. When we move not out of guilt, but out of gratitude. When we eat to nourish, not to fill a void. When we rest not because we're exhausted, but because we deserve care.

Your body is not your enemy. It has carried you through everything, quietly, faithfully. Now, it's your turn to offer it love, not conditions. As you shift your thoughts from criticism to compassion, your body will respond kindly.

A Moment to Visualise

Close your eyes. Imagine standing in front of a mirror, not to judge, but to witness. Smile at the reflection. Now picture your body feeling lighter, stronger, more energised. See yourself dancing freely, moving with ease, breathing deeply.

Let your body speak: "Thank you for not giving up on me." And you, gently respond: "I love you. Let's grow into our best together."

Repeat softly: *"I choose to feel good in my body. I treat it with love, and it rewards me with strength."*

Today's Affirmations

1. **"I listen to my body's needs and respond with kindness."**
2. **"My body deserves love, not punishment."**
3. **"I let go of what no longer serves my health and peace."**
4. **"Every conscious choice I make is a step toward a lighter, happier me."**
5. **"I move my body joyfully because it feels good to be alive."**
6. **"Progress is not perfection, it's showing up for myself, daily."**
7. **"Food is nourishment, not shame. Movement is celebration, not a chore."**

8. **"I release old beliefs about my body and welcome a fresh, loving perspective."**
9. **"I trust my body to transform in its own perfect timing."**
10. **"I am becoming the healthiest version of myself, with ease and grace."**

🌿 One Small Step

Today, choose to move your body in a way that feels joyful, not forced. Walk, stretch, dance in your room, or simply sway to music. While you move, repeat: ***"This body is a gift. I honour it by moving with love."*** Feel the shift. Feel the release.

🙏 A Note to Close With

You are not just losing weight, you are shedding shame, guilt, and outdated stories. This journey isn't about becoming someone new. It's about *remembering* who you already are, whole, powerful, radiant.

"Loving my body is not the reward. It is the first step."

📓 Your Reflection Space

....

....

....

....

4. Manifesting My Dream Home - A Space that Reflects My Soul

"Home isn't a place. It's a feeling, a reflection of who I truly am."

A Personal Insight

The idea of a dream home is more than a wish for walls and windows. It's a longing for sanctuary, a place where you feel safe, at peace, and completely yourself.

Your dream home is already alive within your imagination. It may be surrounded by trees or filled with laughter and light. It could be cosy and minimal, or vibrant and full of life. Whatever shape it takes, the energy behind it is always the same: *belonging*.

When you begin to see your current space with love, whether it's perfect or not, you invite your dream home closer. Manifestation doesn't begin with bricks and blueprints. It begins with alignment, clarity, and gratitude.

What you nurture in your heart, life will build around you.

A Moment to Visualise

Close your eyes. Picture yourself walking into your dream home. The door opens, and the space welcomes you. What do you see? Soft light? Earthy tones? Open windows? Imagine touching the walls, smelling the calm, hearing the quiet joy inside.

Now see yourself living in this space, reading your favourite book, sharing a warm meal, waking up to sunlight. Feel the warmth. Feel the peace. This space is already yours.

Repeat softly: *"I am ready to live in a space that reflects my energy and nurtures my soul."*

Today's Affirmations

1. **"My dream home is not just a place, it is an extension of my soul."**
2. **"I welcome a living space that mirrors my inner peace and joy."**
3. **"Every small corner I care for today leads me closer to the home I envision."**
4. **"My surroundings are becoming more aligned with who I am."**
5. **"I trust life to bring me the right space at the right time."**
6. **"I create beauty, peace, and order in the space I have now."**
7. **"The energy of home lives within me wherever I go."**

8. **"I am grateful for my current shelter and open to more."**
9. **"I walk toward my dream home with clarity, faith, and joy."**
10. **"The home I desire is already being prepared for me in unseen ways."**

🌿 One Small Step

Today, choose one corner of your current space and make it sacred. Clean it, add something beautiful, light a candle, or place a plant there. As you do, say: ***"This reflects the home I am creating. Thank you."*** Let that space hold your vision.

🙏 A Note to Close With

Our homes don't just house our bodies. They hold our energy, our dreams, and the quiet in-between moments that define our days. Every time you choose peace over pressure, simplicity over chaos, or gratitude over restlessness, you're already building your dream home.

"Wherever I go, I carry my sense of home within me-calm, grounded, and full of light."

📔 Your Reflection Space

....

....

....

....

5. Manifesting My Dream Car - Driving My Journey with Confidence

"I am the driver of my destiny, and my journey unfolds with freedom and purpose."

A Personal Insight

A car isn't just a vehicle, it's a symbol of direction, movement, and independence. Manifesting your dream car is about much more than brand or luxury. It's about stepping into a version of yourself who knows where they're going and enjoys the ride.

Maybe it's the smooth drive down a quiet road, music playing. Maybe it's the sense of freedom to go where you choose. Or maybe it's the feeling of having something that reflects your growth, your dream, made real.

When we align with that energy, freedom, worthiness, confidence, the path opens. Life meets us where we are and moves us closer to what we see in our hearts.

A Moment to Visualise

Close your eyes and imagine unlocking your dream car. Slide into the driver's seat. Touch the steering wheel. Feel the comfort, the style, the ease. Take a deep breath as you drive smoothly, calm, with the wind brushing your thoughts away.

You're not in a hurry. You're aligned. See yourself arriving where you want to be, not just in your destination, but in your spirit.

Repeat softly: "I move forward with clarity and joy. I am guided, grounded, and free."

Today's Affirmations

1. **"I am ready to drive my dreams into reality."**
2. **"I attract the perfect vehicle that matches my needs, joy, and energy."**
3. **"Every journey I take is filled with purpose and peace."**
4. **"I am worthy of comfort, style, and freedom on the road."**
5. **"My dream car is a reflection of my progress and potential."**
6. **"I trust the timing and path that lead me to my desires."**
7. **"Each mile I travel brings me closer to who I'm becoming."**

8. **“I am the driver of my story, confident, calm, and in control.”**
9. **“The road ahead is smooth, open, and guided.”**
10. **“I celebrate the freedom to go where I choose, in the vehicle of my dreams.”**

🌿 One Small Step

Sit in your current car or visualise your dream one. Touch the steering wheel (real or imagined) and say: ***“Thank you for carrying me forward. I trust the path ahead.”*** Drive (or walk) today with intention, like you already have what you desire.

🙏 A Note to Close With

Our lives are full of motion, some fast, some slow. Your dream car is not just a destination; it’s part of how you move through life. Let it be a reminder that you are always capable of taking the next step.

“My journey is my own, and I move through it with grace, gratitude, and joy.”

📓 Your Reflection Space

....

....

....

....

6. Manifesting Spiritual Connection and God's Vision

"I align with divine wisdom and walk the path of soulful purpose."

A Personal Insight

Spirituality is not about rituals; it's about recognition. It's recognising that you are not alone, that there is something greater than yourself guiding you. Life flows more smoothly when you trust, surrender, and act with awareness of this greater presence. When I connected with a higher power, I didn't just pray, I listened. I opened my heart to divine guidance and allowed myself to be led. I felt protected and supported, knowing that every step I took was part of a larger plan.

This connection transformed my journey, giving it meaning beyond mere achievements. It wasn't about success or failure, but about growth, purpose, and alignment with a higher truth. Spirituality became a quiet but constant source of strength and direction, helping me navigate life's challenges with grace and confidence, knowing that I was always held.

A Moment to Visualise

Imagine sitting in silence, surrounded by peace. A soft light within your glows, warm and comforting, as you feel the presence of something greater watching over you. In this stillness, you sense a gentle guidance, reassuring you that you are never alone.

Every breath you take deepens your connection, allowing trust and serenity to flow through you, grounding you in love and purpose.

Repeat softly: "I am connected to divine energy. I live my life in sacred alignment."

Today's Affirmations

1. **"I trust the divine timing of my life."**
2. **"I walk with purpose, guided by grace."**
3. **"My intuition is my divine compass."**
4. **"I surrender control and embrace flow."**
5. **"I am safe, seen, and supported by the universe."**
6. **"I honour the sacred in everyday life."**
7. **"My soul is in constant communion with the divine."**
8. **"I see God's vision reflected in my actions."**
9. **"I make decisions from faith, not fear."**
10. **"I live a life of meaning, peace, and inner truth."**

🌿 One Small Step

Spend five minutes today in silent prayer or journaling. Ask with an open heart, listen with patience, and receive the guidance that comes. Allow yourself to be present in the stillness, trusting the process.

Say softly: "In stillness, I ask, listen, and trust. I open my heart to the guidance that flows."

🙏 A Note to Close With

The divine isn't distant, it's within you. You don't need to chase God's light. All you need to do is remember that you carry it inside you, shining brightly through your actions, thoughts, and heart.

"Your soul speaks softly, listen with love."

📔 Your Reflection Space

....

....

....

....

7. Manifesting Inner Peace Amidst Chaos

"I remain calm, centered, and in control no matter what unfolds outside."

A Personal Insight

Peace isn't found in perfect situations; it's born from practice within. I once believed peace was something to be found, an external destination to reach. Now I know it's something I choose, moment by moment, breath by breath. It's a conscious decision to cultivate stillness, even when life is chaotic. Even during life's storms, I've realised that stillness is always within reach.

True peace doesn't depend on silence around you; it's about creating silence within you. When you embrace that inner calm, you can weather any storm. It's the stillness of your mind, the quiet of your heart, that anchors you amidst the turbulence of life. Peace comes when you trust in your ability to remain centred, no matter what's happening around you. It's an ongoing practice, and with each breath, you strengthen your connection to it.

A Moment to Visualise

Close your eyes and picture yourself surrounded by swirling noise or tension. Despite the chaos, at your core, you are still safe and rooted. With each deep breath, you centre yourself, and peace begins to bloom within you, radiating calm throughout your being. During turmoil, your inner stillness remains unwavering, a constant source of strength and serenity.

Repeat softly: "I am centred, calm, and in control of my response."

Today's Affirmations

1. **"I choose peace over panic."**
2. **"My breath anchors me in every moment."**
3. **"No outside situation can disturb my inner stillness."**
4. **"I am grounded even when life is unsettled."**
5. **"I release control and embrace calm."**
6. **"I protect my peace fiercely and lovingly."**
7. **"My energy radiates serenity."**
8. **"I find refuge in silence and self-awareness."**
9. **"I respond with grace, not reactivity."**
10. **"I am the calm in every storm."**

🌿 One Small Step

Take a quiet walk without your phone or distractions. Simply be with yourself and your breath, allowing your mind to clear and your body to reconnect with the present moment. Embrace the peace of solitude.

Say softly: ***"In the quiet, I reconnect with myself, finding peace in each breath and step."***

🙏 A Note to Close With

Your peace is your power. Guard it fiercely, nurture it daily, and return to it often. In moments of stillness, you reconnect with your strength, allowing you to face life's challenges with calm and clarity.

"In the chaos of life, your breath is your sanctuary."

📓 Your Reflection Space

....

....

....

....

8. Manifesting Unshakeable Self-Worth

"I am worthy as I am, nothing to prove, everything to be."

A Personal Insight

Self-worth isn't earned through achievements; it's remembered through presence. I used to tie my value to success, external validation, or how others saw me. I believed that only by accomplishing more or seeking approval could I feel truly worthy. But now, I simply know that I am enough, just as I am. You are born worthy.

Your worth isn't something to be earned or chased; it is something to be claimed and embraced. The world will mirror back to you what you believe about yourself. When you recognise your intrinsic value, you stop searching for validation outside of yourself. Instead, you radiate self-assurance, and that confidence attracts opportunities, respect, and love. You are worthy of all that you desire, simply because you exist. Claim your worth, for it is your birthright.

🌈 A Moment to Visualise

See yourself standing tall, free from comparison and insecurity. There is only peace in who you are. You look in the mirror, not just at your reflection, but deeply into your essence, recognising the strength, beauty, and worth that have always been within you. You are enough, just as you are.

Repeat softly: *"I am enough. I always have been."*

✨ Today's Affirmations

1. **"My worth is inherent, not conditional."**
2. **"I belong, exactly as I am."**
3. **"I release self-doubt and embrace self-respect."**
4. **"I honour my uniqueness and strengths."**
5. **"I am proud of who I'm becoming."**
6. **"I choose to treat myself with kindness."**
7. **"I deserve love, joy, and abundance."**
8. **"I let go of others' opinions of me."**
9. **"I am whole without needing to be fixed."**
10. **"I know my worth, and I live from it."**

🌿 One Small Step

Write a list of 10 things you love about yourself. Speak to them aloud, honouring each one as a sacred truth. Let them sink in, embracing your unique worth.

Say softly: "I celebrate my truth, my essence, and my worth."

🙏 A Note to Close With

You are already enough. Let that truth be your starting point, not your destination. From this place of wholeness, move forward with confidence, knowing that everything you need to grow is already within you.

"When you know your worth, you stop negotiating with fear."

📔 Your Reflection Space

....

....

....

....

9. Manifesting a Life of Emotional Freedom

"I let go of burdens, forgive with ease, and feel safe in my truth."

A Personal Insight

Emotional freedom doesn't mean never feeling pain, it means not being owned by it. It's about choosing how long you hold on to the hurt and having the courage to release what no longer serves you. True freedom comes when we stop letting our emotions control us and instead take charge of how we respond. I used to think forgiveness was about the other person. Now, I understand that it's about finding peace within myself. Letting go isn't just for the sake of others; it's an act of deep love and self-care.

Forgiveness frees us from the burden of anger, resentment, and regret, allowing us to move forward. It's in this release that we find healing, reclaim our power, and create space for inner peace and joy to flourish. Letting go is the key to emotional liberation.

A Moment to Visualise

Visualise the weightlifting from your shoulders as you exhale deeply. With each breath, you gently let go of a thought, memory, or resentment that no longer serves you. Feel the lightness in your body, the freedom in your mind, as you release what holds you back, making space for peace, clarity, and emotional freedom.

Repeat softly: "I am free from emotional chains. I choose peace over pain."

Today's Affirmations

1. **"I release the need to carry past pain."**
2. **"I forgive because I deserve peace."**
3. **"My heart is open and light."**
4. **"I acknowledge my emotions without judgment."**
5. **"I let go with grace and self-respect."**
6. **"I allow space for new joy to enter."**
7. **"I am no longer defined by past wounds."**
8. **"I am whole, healed, and at ease."**
9. **"I free others from my expectations."**
10. **"I live with emotional clarity and calm."**

🌿 One Small Step

Write a release letter to someone or something that has been holding you back. Pour out your emotions, acknowledging the hurt or burden, and then release it. Even if you never send it, feel the weight lift.

Say softly: "I release what no longer serves me, making space for peace and growth."

🙏 A Note to Close With

Letting go doesn't mean you forget. It means you've remembered your worth, realising that you deserve peace, growth, and the freedom to move forward without carrying what no longer serves your journey.

"Emotional freedom begins the moment you stop needing to be understood."

📓 Your Reflection Space

....

....

....

....

10. Manifesting the Confidence to Speak Your Truth

"I honour my voice, value my thoughts, and express myself without fear."

A Personal Insight

For years, I held my truth quietly, thinking silence was safer. But the day I spoke up, with clarity and kindness, I felt my spirit expand. I realised that speaking your truth is not rebellion, it's liberation. It's the act of freeing yourself from the weight of unspoken thoughts and embracing your authentic voice.

Truth doesn't have to be loud; it just has to be real. It's not about seeking validation or approval, but about honouring who you are, unapologetically. When you tell the truth, you stop shrinking to fit in and start growing into the person you're meant to be. Choosing authenticity over approval allows you to step into your full power, and in that, you find peace.

A Moment to Visualise

Visualise yourself in a moment when speaking up feels difficult. You take a deep breath, grounding yourself, and then speak from your heart. As your words flow, you feel heard, respected, and understood. The weight lifts off your shoulders, and you experience a sense of freedom, knowing that your truth is now shared.

Repeat softly: "I speak with courage, kindness, and confidence."

Today's Affirmations

1. **"My voice matters."**
2. **"I express myself honestly and respectfully."**
3. **"I trust what I know and what I feel."**
4. **"I communicate clearly, calmly, and with confidence."**
5. **"I release the fear of judgment."**
6. **"Every time I speak my truth, I become stronger."**
7. **"My truth deserves space and expression."**
8. **"I am authentic in every interaction."**
9. **"I feel empowered when I express myself fully."**
10. **"I allow others to see my truth."**

🌿 One Small Step

Say something today you've been holding in. Start small but let it out with love and honesty. Speaking your truth, no matter how simple, is a step toward freeing your heart.

Say softly: "I release what's been held inside with compassion and courage."

🙏 A Note to Close With

Your voice is a powerful expression of your soul. Don't whisper your truth, let it breathe, speak it boldly and clearly, for it carries the essence of who you are and the strength within you.

"Your truth doesn't need permission, just your presence."

📔 Your Reflection Space

....

....

....

....

Healing and Cultivating Peace

11. Healing and Strengthening My Bond with My Mother

"Through understanding and grace, I mend the roots that raised me."

A Personal Insight

Our relationship with our mother is the first mirror we look into, sometimes clear, sometimes clouded. Whether it's filled with warmth or woven with pain, this bond shapes the way we love, trust, and see ourselves.

Healing this connection is not always about rewriting the past. It's about softening the heart, opening space, and allowing peace to grow where distance once lived. Maybe your relationship with your mother is close. Maybe it's strained, or absent. Whatever the history, what matters now is your willingness to choose compassion, for her, and for yourself.

When we begin to see our mothers not as perfect beings, but as women with their own stories, wounds, and sacrifices, we allow healing to begin, not just between us, but within us.

A Moment to Visualise

Close your eyes. Picture your mother standing before you, at any age that feels right. Imagine holding her hands. Feel her energy. Maybe it's love. Maybe it's tension. Just notice.

Now, take a deep breath and say silently: **"I see you. I release the pain. I invite \ peace between us."** Let a warm light expand from your chest to hers. Even if she's not with you, let that light travel.

Repeat softly... "I forgive, I understand, I open my heart to healing."

Today's Affirmations

1. **"I honour my mother for the life she gave me."**
2. **"I release old wounds and welcome emotional peace."**
3. **"I choose compassion over judgment, understanding over blame."**
4. **"Even in silence, healing can take place."**
5. **"I see the strength and softness that live in us both."**
6. **"I send love to my mother, wherever she may be, in distance, in spirit, or in memory."**
7. **"I allow myself to grieve, to forgive, and to grow."**
8. **"My heart is open to a new chapter with my mother."**

9. **"I carry the wisdom of my lineage with pride and peace."**
10. **"As I heal this bond, I nurture the mother within me."**

🌿 One Small Step

Today, write a short note or message to your mother. If she is no longer alive or reachable, write it anyway. Speak from the heart. Express gratitude, forgiveness, or whatever is true for you. Then, fold it gently and keep it somewhere sacred or let it go.

🙏 A Note to Close With

Healing your relationship with your mother doesn't mean forgetting the pain. It means holding space for both love and truth. Whether you continue the relationship, redefine it, or simply bless it from afar, know this: you are not broken. You are becoming whole.

"I hold the parts of my mother that made me, and the parts I chose to grow beyond, with equal grace."

📓 Your Reflection Space

....

....

....

....

12. Healing and Respecting My Relationship with My Father

"In honoring the man who shaped my strength, I reclaim my power and peace."

A Personal Insight

A father's presence or his absence leaves a mark on the way we see ourselves and navigate the world. Sometimes that mark is shaped by guidance and strength. Sometimes by silence, distance, or wounds left unspoken. Healing the father-child relationship is not about rewriting the story. It's about creating a new chapter, from a place of maturity, understanding, and deep self-love.

Fathers, too, are human. They carry generational pressure, hidden emotions, and untold stories. When we begin to look beyond the surface, space opens. And in that space, healing can begin, not just for the bond, but for your own masculine/feminine balance. Releasing the weight of blame allows you to walk lighter in your own identity.

A Moment to Visualise

Sit quietly. Imagine your father as he was when you were a child. Then imagine him as he is now or was, in your last memory. Breathe deeply and imagine a warm, grounding energy connecting you both, not of expectation, but of acknowledgement.

Repeat softly… *"I free myself from the past. I choose peace with my father."*

Today's Affirmations

1. **"I accept my father's journey, even if I don't fully understand it."**
2. **"I release the need for approval and grow in self-respect."**
3. **"I choose healing over holding on to hurt."**
4. **"I allow compassion to soften any lingering pain."**
5. **"I see the human behind the role of 'father.'"**
6. **"I welcome clarity, forgiveness, and emotional freedom."**
7. **"Our past may be imperfect, but my healing is intentional."**
8. **"I carry forward the strength I inherited, leaving behind the struggle."**
9. **"Even in distance or silence, I can send peace."**

10. "My relationship with my father evolves as I evolve."

🌿 One Small Step

Write down one positive or painful lesson that your father taught you. Reflect on how it shaped you. Then write a single line of gratitude or closure beneath it. Fold it and place it somewhere private or burn it safely as a ritual of release.

Say silently: "*You are part of my story. I released the pain. I honour the lessons.*" *Let go of what no longer needs to be carried.*

🙏 A Note to Close With

You don't need the past to be perfect to heal. All you need is the courage to soften the edges and reclaim your peace. As you restore this bond, whether memory or spirit, you make space for healthier relationships in every other part of your life.

"Healing my relationship with my father gave me strength, not to be like him, but to be more fully myself."

📓 Your Reflection Space

....

....

....

....

13. Nurturing Harmony in My Relationship with Wife / Husband

"Where love leads, ego dissolves. Where understanding grows, connection deepens."

A Personal Insight

Relationships aren't meant to be perfect. They are meant to be real, evolving, and sacred in their own way. When we enter a union, we do so not just with love, but with expectations, past wounds, and unspoken desires.

The secret isn't in finding a flawless partner; it's in choosing each other again and again, even on the days when love feels like work.

Harmony in a relationship comes when we replace control with curiosity, blame with compassion, and assumption with open-hearted dialogue. When you lead with a presence instead of pride, your partner feels seen, not just for who they are, but for who they're becoming. Manifesting peace in your relationship begins with the question: *Am I choosing to love today?*

A Moment to Visualise

Close your eyes. Picture you and your partner in a space of ease, no conflict, no pressure. Just two souls resting in each other's presence. Imagine holding hands, smiling softly, saying something kind and unfiltered. Feel what it's like to hear. To be embraced without needing to explain. See your partner not as someone to fix, but as someone to understand.

Repeat softly… *"I choose connection. I choose calm. I choose us, with love."*

Today's Affirmations

1. **"I see my partner through the eyes of compassion, not criticism."**
2. **"Our relationship is a space of growth, not perfection."**
3. **"I express my needs with love and listen with presence."**
4. **"We release the past and create new harmony, together."**
5. **"Every challenge we face is an invitation to deepen our bond."**
6. **"I honour the love that first brought us together."**
7. **"I choose patience when it's easier to react."**
8. **"Our connection is guided by trust, kindness, and care."**

9. **"We speak with respect, even when we disagree."**

10. **"Love is our language. Peace is our practice."**

🌿 One Small Step

Write a short note, text, or letter to your partner today, just a few words of appreciation. Something real, something now. Even if there has been distance, take the first step with love.

Say: ***"Thank you for showing up in this journey with me. I see you. I'm grateful for you."***

🙏 A Note to Close With

Intimacy doesn't grow from grand displays; it's nurtured in the quiet, everyday moments. A gentle glance, a kind word, a shared silence, or simply the patience to understand one another. These small acts, repeated with care, build a deep, lasting connection. When love is tended to regularly, it blossoms into something rare, resilient, and truly extraordinary.

> ***"Peace with my partner begins in me. The love we share grows with every conscious choice I make."***

📔 Your Reflection Space

…………………………………………………………………

…………………………………………………………………

…………………………………………………………………

…………………………………………………………………

14. Manifesting the Path to Becoming the Best Son

"I carry forward my family's values with gratitude, honour, and strength."

A Personal Insight

Being a good son isn't just about fulfilling expectations; it's about living with integrity, showing up with respect, and honouring the roots that shaped you. It's about recognising the sacrifices made for you and carrying that legacy forward with gratitude. Being a son means holding space for your parents' wisdom while building your own future.

I've come to understand that every parent longs not for perfection, but for presence, the presence of a son who listens, learns, and leads by example. It's not about grand gestures, but the daily choices to be there, to show respect, and to be a steady source of love and support. Through these actions, you honour the foundation they've given you while creating a life that reflects the values they instilled. A son's presence is the greatest gift he can give.

🌈 A Moment to Visualise

Picture yourself sitting with your parents, offering your time, attention, and love. As you listen and share in their presence, their eyes shine not just with pride, but with peace, knowing that you value them and the bond you share. In these moments, you bring them comfort, showing that their love and wisdom are cherished deeply.

Repeat softly: *"I respect my roots. I grow with gratitude."*

💥 Today's Affirmations

1. **"I honour my parents through my actions and words."**
2. **"I communicate with patience and openness."**
3. **"I carry our traditions with pride and love."**
4. **"I learn from their stories and wisdom."**
5. **"I support them emotionally and practically."**
6. **"I reflect the values they planted in me."**
7. **"I am present in both joy and challenge."**
8. **"My journey uplifts our legacy."**
9. **"I am the son they prayed for."**
10. **"I am proud of the bond we nurture."**

🌿 One Small Step

Call or visit your parents today, even if only for a few minutes. Take the time to ask them about something that matters to them and listen with genuine interest. It's these small moments that strengthen your bond and show them they are valued.

Say softly: ***"Today, I choose to connect deeply with my parents and honour their hearts."***

🙏 A Note to Close With

A son becomes a man not by age, but by honouring those who shaped him with gratitude. It's through respect, appreciation, and understanding that he matures, carrying the lessons and love of his roots forward.

"Your roots are not your anchors, they're your foundation."

📔 Your Reflection Space

....

....

....

....

15. Manifesting the Grace of Being the Best Daughter

"I honour my parents with kindness, compassion, and conscious presence."

A Personal Insight

Being a daughter is a dance of love, responsibility, and strength. It's about caring for those who have cared for you, learning from their wisdom, and continuing the circle of grace they've set in motion. The best daughters aren't necessarily the most obedient; they are the most understanding, able to see beyond expectations and recognise the deeper needs of their parents.

I've realised that our parents don't just need our help, they need our time, respect, and gentle acknowledgement of their sacrifices. It's in the small acts of love, the moments spent listening, and the appreciation shown for their life's work that we truly honour them. As daughters, our role is not only to receive love but to give it back with gratitude and understanding. It's through these actions that we build lasting, meaningful connections with those who shaped us.

A Moment to Visualise

Imagine hugging your mother or father, feeling their breath slow with peace as they rest in your embrace. In this moment, you realise you are their anchor, their safe place amidst life's challenges.

Your presence brings them comfort, knowing that their love has shaped you into someone they can rely on, trust, and be proud of. The roles may shift, but the bond of love remains constant, unbreakable, and deeply fulfilling.

Repeat softly: *"I am my parents' light and strength."*

✵ Today's Affirmations

1. **"I give back to my parents with joy and humility."**
2. **"I speak with love and listen with patience."**
3. **"I understand their fears and cherish their dreams."**
4. **"I balance my freedom with family values."**
5. **"I am a source of strength in their ageing years."**
6. **"I carry their legacy with grace."**
7. **"I care with devotion, not duty."**
8. **"I celebrate our bond every day."**
9. **"I show up in ways that matter to them."**
10. **"I am a daughter they are proud to call their own."**

🌿 One Small Step

Sit with your parents today and ask them what made them happiest this week. Take a moment to listen, appreciate their joy, and connect with the little things that brighten their lives. It's a simple way to show care.

Say softly: ***"Today, I choose to connect with my parents and cherish their happiness, no matter how small."***

🙏 A Note to Close With

Daughters are the threads that sew generations together, creating a bond that transcends time. Your love is the finest weaves, connecting hearts and preserving the strength, wisdom, and beauty passed down through the generations.

"A daughter is not just born, she's built through presence and love."

📔 Your Reflection Space

....

....

....

....

16. Cultivating Joy and Respect with My Son and Daughter

"In loving them as individuals, I help them love themselves. In respecting who they are, I help them rise."

A Personal Insight

Raising a son and a daughter together is a dance of balance, equal in love, but unique in language. Each child arrives with their own temperament, sensitivities, and spark. What comforts one may challenge the other. What inspires one may confuse the other. But the thread that connects them, and you, is love grounded in respect.

To parents, with the intention is to listen more than you speak, to see beyond behaviours into emotions, and to offer your presence as a shelter. It's understanding that equality doesn't mean sameness, it means honouring each child for their distinct identity and rhythm. They may walk different paths, but the roots come from you. And when those roots are nourished with joy, trust, and empathy, they grow into adults who know how to love and be loved.

A Moment to Visualise

Close your eyes. Picture your son and daughter, together or individually. See them laughing, learning, growing in their own way. See yourself beside them, not leading or pushing, but walking *with* them. Imagine the love between you as a glowing thread, strong, flexible, and full of light. Let that love expand, reaching every corner of your connection.

Repeat softly… *"I nurture both with open eyes, open arms, and open heart."*

Today's Affirmations

1. **"I honour the differences in my son and daughter and celebrate them equally."**
2. **"I speak to each of them in the language their heart understands."**
3. **"My love is not measured; it flows fully and freely to both."**
4. **"I hold space for their emotions, even when they express them differently."**
5. **"I am building a family where joy, respect, and empathy are the foundation."**
6. **"I lead with values, not control, with care, not comparison."**
7. **"I am present for their growth, mistakes, and victories without judgment."**
8. **"Our relationship is a haven where they can be fully themselves."**

9. **“I trust them to become exactly who they are meant to be.”**

10. **“Each day, I plant seeds of confidence, kindness, and connection.”**

🌿 One Small Step

Today, take a moment with each child, individually. One sentence, one smile, one shared moment. Say something specific that affirms *who they are*, not just what they do. Example: ***“I love how your mind works.”*** *or* ***“You light up a room just by being in it.”***

🙏 A Note to Close With

You’re not here to mould them into each other or into you. You are here to guide them into themselves. And your love, your presence, your quiet belief in them… those will echo long after the words are forgotten.

“My greatest gift to my children is seeing them clearly, loving them freely, and trusting their journey completely.”

📓 Your Reflection Space

....

....

....

....

17. Manifesting the Bond of a Trustworthy Friend

"I am loyal, present, and a safe space for the hearts I hold."

A Personal Insight

True friendship isn't measured by how often you talk; it's about how deeply you understand one another. A trustworthy friend is someone whose presence brings a sense of safety, whose words have the power to heal, and whose silence provides support when needed. I've discovered that to be a great friend, you don't need all the answers. What matters is that you care, you show up, and you love without expecting anything in return.

Trust is not built through grand gestures, but through consistent acts of kindness, patience, and understanding. It's in the quiet moments of connection, in the laughter shared, and in the ability to be present during the tough times. A true friend doesn't just listen; they make you feel heard, valued, and never alone. Friendship is about being there, not just for the good times, but for everything in between.

A Moment to Visualise

Visualise a friend leaning on your shoulder, sharing laughter or opening up about a fear. In that moment, feel your presence becoming their peace, a safe space where they can be vulnerable and supported. Your understanding and care create quiet comfort, reminding them that they are not alone. Your friendship is a steady anchor, offering warmth and strength when it's needed most.

Repeat softly: *"I am a loyal friend. I offer strength, truth, and joy."*

Today's Affirmations

1. **"I am dependable and understanding."**
2. **"I listen with empathy and without judgment."**
3. **"I honour my friends' truths and dreams."**
4. **"My presence brings comfort and warmth."**
5. **"I celebrate my friends' wins as my own."**
6. **"I am honest, kind, and emotionally available."**
7. **"I grow through meaningful connections."**
8. **"I make time for those I care about."**
9. **"I support in silence and celebrate in sound."**
10. **"I am proud to be a trustworthy friend."**

🪶 One Small Step

Reach out to a friend today just to say, ***"I appreciate you."*** A simple message can brighten their day and remind them how much they are valued, strengthening the bond of your friendship.

🙏 A Note to Close With

Friendship is the family we choose, and being a safe space for someone is the highest gift you can offer. It's in unconditional support, understanding, and love that true connections are made and cherished.

"The best friendships are not kept, they are nurtured."

📔 Your Reflection Space

....

....

....

....

18. Embracing My Relationship with My Mother-in-Law with Grace

"In understanding her journey, I find peace in mine. In offering grace, I grow in love."

A Personal Insight

The relationship with a mother-in-law can be tender, layered, and sometimes challenging. It holds within it the echoes of generations, traditions, expectations, love, and sometimes, silent tension. Whether this bond feels close or distant, easy or difficult, it offers us a powerful opportunity: to lead with grace, to love without losing ourselves, and to understand without always needing to agree.

You don't have to be perfect. Neither does she. But if you can meet her with soft edges and an open heart, you'll find yourself healing more than just a relationship; you'll be healing generations. Respect doesn't mean surrendering your truth. It means choosing peace over pride and wisdom over reaction.

A Moment to Visualise

Close your eyes. Picture your mother-in-law, not through history, but through the heart. Imagine her life, her challenges, her hopes. See her not just as a figure in your family, but as a woman with her own story. Now, imagine sharing a quiet cup of tea. No words. Just a moment of silent respect. Feel the warmth between you, genuine, even if imperfect.

Repeat softly… *"I send peace between us. I hold space for understanding."*

Today's Affirmations

1. **"I meet my mother-in-law with patience, not expectation."**
2. **"I release the past and create a new path with kindness."**
3. **"Our bond is growing with grace, one day at a time."**
4. **"I honour her role in my family's story."**
5. **"Peace begins in me, and it ripples outward."**
6. **"I choose boundaries that honour love and self-respect."**
7. **"My words are gentle, and my energy is calm."**
8. **"Every woman deserves understanding, including her and me."**

9. **"I grow stronger by choosing compassion over judgment."**

10. **"I am open to a relationship rooted in mutual respect."**

🪶 One Small Step

Today, send her a small note, spoken, written, or in thought. It doesn't need to be long. Just a sentence of peace, gratitude, or goodwill. Even if words aren't possible, offer her kindness in your heart. Let it go. Let it soften you.

Say softly: ***"With grace in my heart, I send you peace and kindness."***

🙏 A Note to Close With

Not every connection becomes close. But every connection offers growth. As you honour this bond with grace and strength, you become a reflection of the peace you wish to see in your family.

"I walk with grace through this shared path. I choose love, even when it's quiet."

📔 Your Reflection Space

....

....

....

....

19. Cultivating Peace with My Father-in-law

"I welcome respect where connection may be quiet, and I offer peace where words may be few."

A Personal Insight

The relationship with a father-in-law can often be quiet, less spoken, more felt. It may not always carry warmth at first glance, but it holds the potential for mutual respect, understanding, and quiet trust. Sometimes, this bond is built on shared moments. Sometimes it's bridged through distance and observation. But at its heart, it's a connection between two people navigating family, values, and space.

You don't need to force closeness. You only need to hold space for respect, empathy, and open-hearted boundaries. And in that space, healing can occur, often silently, often slowly, but always meaningfully. When you release expectations and honour both your truth and his presence, you create peace that speaks louder than words.

A Moment to Visualise

Close your eyes. Imagine your father-in-law, not just as a title, but as a man shaped by his life, his era, his experiences. Now, imagine sitting beside him, calm, present, no pressure to speak. Feel the quiet connection building. See mutual respect growing like a tree between you, slow but rooted. No need to change each other. Just a shared ground of family.

Repeat softly… *"I choose peace in this bond. I allow respect to guide our path."*

Today's Affirmations

1. **"I honour my father-in-law's journey and offer him space to be seen."**
2. **"Our connection is growing in its own time and way."**
3. **"I release expectations and embrace quiet understanding."**
4. **"Respect flows both ways when given with sincerity."**
5. **"I choose patience in moments of difference."**
6. **"I am creating peace in my family through presence, not pressure."**
7. **"I give what I wish to receive: kindness, respect, openness."**
8. **"It's okay if our bond is quiet, as long as it is real."**

9. **"I see strength in choosing love where distance once lived."**
10. **"This relationship is not a duty, it is an opportunity for grace."**

🌿 One Small Step

If possible, acknowledge him today with a small gesture, eye contact, a smile, or a genuine greeting. If not in person, send him a silent blessing: ***"May we both be free from judgment and full of calm respect."***

🙏 A Note to Close With

Peace doesn't always come in big conversations. Sometimes, it arrives in small acknowledgements, in simply choosing not to carry old tension into a new moment. Let this relationship unfold on its own timeline. Your openness already changes its direction.

"I honor this bond, not through effort, but through the quiet grace of respect."

📓 Your Reflection Space

....

....

....

....

Education and Professional Competence

20. Manifesting School Admission with Trust

"The right place for my growth is already opening its doors to me."

A Personal Insight

Applying to schools, whether for your child or yourself, often brings feelings of pressure, uncertainty, and the fear of not being "enough." But education isn't just a race for prestige or rankings; it's an alignment search. The right school is a place that sees potential, encourages individuality, and supports authentic growth. When you release the weight of desperation and embrace trust, the process becomes more peaceful and purposeful.

You begin to believe that the perfect opportunity is already unfolding for you or your child. Every form, interview, and waiting period is part of a greater path, one guided by faith, not fear. Let this chapter be a turning point where you move from stress to surrender. Trust that the right door will open when you show up with heart, hope, and belief in your journey.

A Moment to Visualise

Close your eyes and envision yourself receiving that long-awaited admission letter or hearing the good news. Feel your face light up with a joyful smile, your shoulders drop as relief washes over you, and your breath deepens with ease. Gratitude fills your heart. In this moment, you feel supported by life, confident in your path, and ready to embrace the next chapter. Trust that what's meant for you is already making its way.

Repeat softly... *"I am ready to grow. The right school is ready for me."*

Today's Affirmations

1. **"I am aligned with the school that supports my growth."**
2. **"I trust the admission process is unfolding perfectly."**
3. **"I release fear and welcome ease."**
4. **"I am prepared and deserving of this opportunity."**
5. **"I believe in my abilities and potential."**
6. **"I stay calm while waiting for the right result."**
7. **"I am attracting a place where I feel inspired."**
8. **"The universe is arranging all that I need."**
9. **"What's meant for me will always find me."**

10. **"I am stepping into a new chapter of learning and joy."**

🌿 One Small Step

Write down the name of your dream school on a piece of paper and place it somewhere visible, on your mirror, desk, or journal. Each time you see it, take a moment to pause, breathe, and **say softly: *"You are already mine in spirit. I am aligned, I am ready, I am worthy."*** Let this affirmation anchor your belief and guide your energy each day. Trust that what you desire is already reaching back toward you.

🙏 A Note to Close With

You are not simply waiting, you are actively preparing, growing, and aligning with what's meant for you. The school you dream of isn't just a goal; it's a match seeking someone exactly like you. Let faith, not fear, lead the way. Each step forward is a sign that you're getting closer to the perfect fit.

"The path to my learning is already open; I simply walk it with trust."

📓 Your Reflection Space

....

....

....

....

21. Manifesting College Admission with Confidence

"I am worthy of the next chapter. I belong where I will grow the most."

A Personal Insight

Getting into college often feels like one of the most defining moments in your academic journey. It can stir up emotions, pressure, excitement, self-doubt, and comparison. But here's an important truth: your worth isn't determined by a school's name, ranking, or prestige. The true value of your education lies in how much you grow, how deeply you learn, and how aligned you feel in your environment.

A place that nurtures your strengths and honours your individuality will serve you far better than one chosen out of pressure or competition. Let go of fear, release the grip of comparison, and trust your own path. When you believe in your readiness and remain open, the right door will open with ease. You don't have to chase approval; you simply align with who you are, and opportunities follow naturally.

A Moment to Visualise

Picture yourself stepping onto a campus that immediately feels like home, where your presence belongs. The air carries a sense of welcome, and each corner reflects possibility. You feel seen for who you truly are, respected for your voice, and energised by the community around you.

With every step, your confidence grows. You're not trying to fit in, you're simply becoming more of yourself. You walk with purpose and peace, knowing you are exactly where you're meant to be.

Repeat softly: *"The right college is already waiting for me. I am ready to rise."*

Today's Affirmations

1. **"I am attracting an academic path that nurtures my potential."**
2. **"I release doubt and welcome clarity."**
3. **"My efforts are enough. My dreams are valid."**
4. **"I stay grounded in calm, not panic."**
5. **"I am capable of achieving what I desire."**
6. **"I remain patient and positive through the process."**
7. **"The admissions I receive are aligned with my growth."**
8. **"I am ready for new challenges and learning."**

9. **"I trust in divine timing and placement."**
10. **"My journey is unfolding just as it should."**

🌿 One Small Step

Write a short, loving message to your future college self and place it somewhere you'll see often: ***"I knew you'd make it. I'm proud of you. You faced every doubt and challenge with courage, earning this moment through resilience and heart. Keep growing, keep shining, and never forget your journey. I'll always be rooting for you."*** Let it be your reminder of strength and purpose every single day.

🙏 A Note to Close With

College is not just a destination; it's the gateway to your next transformation, a space where your passions deepen, and your identity expands. You're not desperately trying to get in; you're aligning with your path, preparing to receive what's already making its way to you. Trust the timing, trust yourself, and let it unfold naturally.

"I don't compete. I align. And what's mine finds me."

📓 Your Reflection Space

....

....

....

....

22. Empowering My Mind – Affirmations for Examination Success

"My calm is my power. My preparation is my strength. I am ready, and I believe in myself."

A Personal Insight

Examinations are often seen as a test of memory or performance, but at their core, they are also a test of self-trust. It's not just about what you know, but how you *feel* when you're asked to show what you know. Success doesn't start on the day of the test. It begins in the quiet moments before, with your mindset, your breath, your belief.

When you study with intention, rest with care, and speak to yourself with kindness, your mind becomes a friend, not a battlefield. The more you affirm your capability, the more your confidence grows, not as ego, but as calm assurance. You are not defined by a grade. You are shaped by your courage, discipline, and the effort you've put in. That's where your real power lies.

A Moment to Visualise

Close your eyes. Imagine yourself sitting in the exam hall. You're prepared. You're calm. You take a deep breath. Your hands are steady, your mind is clear. Now imagine the paper in front of you. You read it with ease. The answers begin to flow. There's no panic, only quiet confidence.

Repeat softly… *"I am focused. I am capable. I am ready."*

Today's Affirmations

1. **"I retain knowledge with ease and recall it with clarity."**
2. **"I remain calm and confident in all exam situations."**
3. **"I trust my preparation and release all fear."**
4. **"My mind works clearly under pressure."**
5. **"Every breath I take grounds and energises me."**
6. **"I focus on what I know, not on what I fear."**
7. **"I am allowed to succeed. I permit myself to shine."**
8. **"I learn from challenges and grow stronger with each test."**
9. **"I am capable, intelligent, and resilient."**
10. **"Success flows to me because I believe in myself."**

🌿 One Small Step

Before you study or begin your test, place your hand over your chest and **say softly: *"I am doing my best. I believe in my efforts. I am more than enough."*** Repeat it once. Then once more. Then begin.

🙏 A Note to Close With

Exams will pass. But what stays with you is the belief you built, the discipline you practised, and the strength you discovered along the way. Grades come and go. Your growth is permanent.

"I honour my journey. I trust my path. And I rise with quiet strength."

📓 Your Reflection Space

....

....

....

....

23. Manifesting Your Dream Job

"I align with a career that fulfils my purpose, passion, and potential."

A Personal Insight

A dream job isn't about landing a position at a famous company or earning a flashy title; it's about finding a space that feels like home to your spirit. It's where your talents are valued, your voice is heard, your creativity is welcomed, and your values are respected. It's where fulfilment, not just a paycheck, meets you at the end of each day. *"I deserve meaningful work. I align, I grow, I attract the career meant for me."*

When I stopped settling for "good enough" and started believing I deserved to feel inspired by my work, something shifted. The right opportunities began to find me. You don't chase a dream job; you grow into the version of yourself that naturally attracts it. It's not about luck; it's about alignment. Your dream role exists, and it's waiting for the most authentic version of you to step forward.

A Moment to Visualise

Imagine walking into an office or creative space that feels like home. The energy aligns with who you are. You're doing work you love, surrounded by people who respect your ideas and value your growth. Every task feels meaningful, every day a step forward. You contribute with confidence and are appreciated for being authentically you. This is more than a job; it's a reflection of your purpose, passion, and potential finally coming together.

Say softly: *"My dream job is seeking me as much as I'm seeking it."*

Today's Affirmations

1. **"I am worthy of fulfilling and joyful work."**
2. **"Opportunities aligned with my gifts are finding me."**
3. **"I attract roles that excite and elevate me."**
4. **"I am prepared, qualified, and confident."**
5. **"The right job flows into my life with ease."**
6. **"My career reflects my purpose and strengths."**
7. **"I grow daily in my field and in myself."**
8. **"My ideal work environment welcomes me."**
9. **"I am grateful for the journey and the offer ahead."**
10. **"I rise into the career I deserve."**

🌿 One Small Step

Take one step today toward the career you envision. Update your resume or connect with someone in a role you admire. Ask questions, stay curious, and move forward with intention. Growth begins with action.

Say softly: ***"I take bold steps. I am moving with purpose. I'm ready."***

🙏 A Note to Close With

You weren't made to work just to survive. You're meant to thrive in work that lights you up, challenges you, and brings you joy. Choose a path that nourishes your soul, not just your schedule.

"The job you dream of already exists. So does the version of you who'll earn it."

📓 Your Reflection Space

....

....

....

....

24. Affirmations for Interview Confidence

"My presence speaks before my words. I walk into opportunity with calm assurance."

A Personal Insight

An interview is not just a conversation; it's a unique opportunity where your presence, experiences, and voice align to create possibility. It's normal to feel the urge to impress or fear making mistakes. But the real impact comes when you let go of pressure and lean into authenticity. You're not expected to perform; you're invited to show up prepared, calm, and true to your goals. Interviews are less about having perfect answers and more about being genuinely present.

When you trust your preparation and speak from a place of clarity and purpose, the right opportunities naturally gravitate toward you. Your story, told with confidence and heart, is your greatest strength. So, step into each interview not to prove your worth, but to share who you already are, grounded, capable, and ready.

🌈 A Moment to Visualise

Close your eyes. Picture yourself stepping into an interview room or joining a video call. Your shoulders are relaxed, and your breath is steady. Confidence radiates through your calm presence. You speak with clarity, ask thoughtful questions, and genuinely connect. The conversation flows with purpose, authenticity, and mutual understanding.

Say softly. *"I am focused, I am prepared, and I am ready to receive what aligns with me."*

🌟 Today's Affirmations

1. **"I walk into interviews with confidence and calm."**
2. **"My energy reflects clarity, focus, and authenticity."**
3. **"I express my value with ease and trust the outcome."**
4. **"I am worthy of roles that match my skills and passion."**
5. **"I allow my voice to be strong, kind, and heard."**
6. **"I attract professional spaces that support my growth."**
7. **"Every interview teaches me, shapes me, and elevates me."**
8. **"I listen deeply and speak from alignment."**

9. **"I am more than enough, just as I am."**
10. **"I trust that the right opportunity is already seeking me."**

🙞 One Small Step

Write down three qualities that make you a valuable contributor in any role. Repeat them out loud while looking in the mirror. Let your confidence be rooted in truth.

Say softly: ***"I honour my strengths, I trust my journey, and I stand in my true worth"***

🙏 A Note to Close With

True power doesn't come from perfection; it comes from presence. You don't need to have it all figured out. Just be fully here, as you are. The right paths, people, and possibilities will naturally align with your energy and recognise the light you carry within.

"I am not trying to get the job; I am aligning with the job that is already mine."

📔 Your Reflection Space

....

....

....

....

25. Manifesting a Purposeful Start-Up

"With each step, I shape a venture that reflects my soul and serves the world."

A Personal Insight

Starting a business isn't just about logos or profits; it's about solving real problems, creating value, and walking in alignment with your unique gifts. A start-up is a brave leap into self-leadership, where you take ownership of your vision and decisions.

When I first embraced my idea, I didn't have all the answers, but I knew I had something worth building. The journey wasn't easy, but every challenge became an opportunity for growth. Every setback or delay wasn't failure; it was a refinement of the vision I was shaping. A start-up is not

Repeat softly… *"I am building a business with purpose, passion, and patience."*

Today's Affirmations

1. **"My start-up is rooted in service and authenticity."**
2. **"I take bold steps toward clarity and creation."**
3. **"Every delay brings me deeper insight."**
4. **"I trust the evolution of my ideas."**

5. **“Support, strategy, and success surround my vision.”**
6. **“I build with integrity and intention.”**
7. **“My work uplifts lives and solves real problems.”**
8. **“I am becoming the leader my vision requires.”**
9. **“I welcome growth, resilience, and recognition.”**
10. **“My business is a blessing in progress.”**

🌿 One Small Step

Write down one product, service, or solution your start-up could offer. Don’t overthink it, just flow with the idea. **Say softly:** ***"I trust my creativity and my ability to bring value to the world."***

🙏 A Note to Close With

You don’t need a perfect blueprint to begin. What you need is faith in your vision, the fire to fuel your passion, and the courage to take the first step. The rest will unfold as you move forward with determination.

“Start-ups are not born from certainty, but from commitment.”

📔 Your Reflection Space

....

....

....

....

26. Manifesting Charisma as an Attractive Spokesperson

"My words are magnetic, my presence is warm, and my truth resonates."

A Personal Insight

Being a powerful spokesperson isn't about delivering perfect lines about showing up with sincerity and conviction. True influence comes not from polished words, but from the passion behind them. The most magnetic speakers aren't flawless; they're deeply aligned with what they believe.

I used to tremble at the thought of public speaking, until I discovered that the goal wasn't to impress others, it was simply to express myself honestly. Once your energy aligns with your intention, your audience doesn't just hear you; they feel you. Authenticity bridges gaps that eloquence never could. It invites hearts to open and ears to truly listen. ***"My voice is enough. My truth is powerful. I speak to connect, not to perform. I trust my message, and I let it move through me."***

A Moment to Visualise

Imagine standing on a stage or at the centre of a meeting room. You speak with clarity, confidence, and heart. Your words aren't just heard, they're felt. People lean in, captivated by your presence. There's no need to force anything; your authenticity does the work. The room responds not to perfection, but to your passion. Your message flows naturally, landing with purpose and power. You're not just speaking; you're making a lasting connection.

Repeat gently... *"I speak with power, warmth, and truth."*

Today's Affirmations

1. **"My voice carries confidence and calm."**
2. **"I express myself clearly and meaningfully."**
3. **"I connect with my audience effortlessly."**
4. **"I am respected and remembered for my message."**
5. **"My presence uplifts the room."**
6. **"I speak not to impress, but to inspire."**
7. **"Words come to me with ease and impact."**
8. **"I am charismatic, composed, and centred."**
9. **"Every time I speak, I grow stronger."**
10. **"My truth is heard and honoured."**

🪶 One Small Step

Record yourself speaking for two minutes about something you love. Watch the playback with compassion, not critique. Notice your unique voice, your expression, your spark. Celebrate the strengths that come naturally to you. Growth begins with acceptance, not judgment. **Say softly: *"I honour my voice. I see my strengths. I grow with kindness."***

🙏 A Note to Close With

Charisma isn't learned, it's remembered. It's the spark you were born with, now expressed through voice.

"Speak with soul, and the world listens in silence."

📔 Your Reflection Space

....

....

....

....

27. Manifesting the Dream to Become a Doctor

"I heal with compassion, serve with purpose, and learn with devotion."

A Personal Insight

To be a doctor is to become a vessel of healing, not just for bodies, but for hearts, lives, and entire families. It's not merely a profession; it's a sacred calling rooted in compassion, courage, and continuous service. The decision to step into medicine is a vow: to never stop learning, to be present in pain, and to offer strength when others feel weak.

When I envisioned myself in this noble role, I saw more than a white coat or a stethoscope. I saw the weight of responsibility, the quiet power of empathy, and the resilience required to walk beside people in their most vulnerable moments. I wasn't just choosing a career; I was answering a deeper calling. *"I choose to heal. I choose to serve. I carry this calling with grace."*

A Moment to Visualise

Visualise yourself in a white coat, stepping into the hospital with calm confidence and purpose. Each step you take carries compassion. You greet patients with warmth, listen with presence, and speak with clarity. In every room, your presence brings comfort, your knowledge offers hope, and your care inspires trust. You are steady in crisis, skilled in action, and kind at heart. You don't just treat symptoms, you uplift lives.

Repeat gently… *"I am a healer. I am becoming the doctor this world needs."*

Today's Affirmations

1. **"I study with dedication and purpose."**
2. **"My hands bring healing; my words bring hope."**
3. **"I learn from every patient and every page."**
4. **"I am committed to excellence and empathy."**
5. **"Challenges strengthen my calling."**
6. **"My mind is sharp, and my heart is soft."**
7. **"I am worthy of this responsibility."**
8. **"The journey to becoming a doctor empowers me."**
9. **"My service creates ripples of healing."**
10. **"I am already the soul of a doctor in action."**

🌿 One Small Step

Spend time exploring a field of medicine that draws your heart. Read, listen, and observe with curiosity. Let your questions lead you deeper. The path will reveal itself not all at once, but step by step, through passion and purpose.

Say softly: *"My curiosity is a compass. I trust it to lead me to my calling."*

🙏 A Note to Close With

Healing isn't just a job, it's a quiet devotion, a promise to show up with heart. If you feel the calling, honour it. Trust that simply feeling it means you've already begun. Feel it: "I am being led by purpose. My path is unfolding with grace."

"To heal even one soul is to fulfil a divine mission."

📔 Your Reflection Space

....

....

....

....

28. Manifesting a Life as a Successful Engineer

"I build solutions, I improve lives, and I innovate with purpose."

A Personal Insight

Engineers don't just build structures; they build solutions. They solve real-world problems with logic, creativity, and precision. From designing cleaner energy systems to creating smarter cities, engineers shape the future with every blueprint and calculation. Engineering is not just about machines and measurements; it's about impact. *"I am a builder of ideas. I engineer change. I turn vision into reality."*

I remember being inspired by bridges stretching across rivers, by the elegance of systems working in harmony, and by the quiet genius behind everyday innovations. I didn't just want to admire those feats; I wanted to contribute. To be a part of that silent force that transforms lives, one design at a time. Becoming an engineer is a commitment to improvement, to think critically, create sustainably, and serve humanity through innovation.

🌈 A Moment to Visualise

Visualise yourself in an engineering lab, on a construction site, or sketch designs on a screen. Feel the focus in your hands, the purpose in your mind. See your ideas take shape, bridges, systems, tools, or code, crafted with precision and care. Watch your creation come to life, solving a real problem, easing someone's struggle, or sparking progress. You're not just building things, you're building futures.

Say Softly… "*I design, I solve, I serve. I am an engineer in spirit and skill.*"

✨ Today's Affirmations

1. **"I am a builder of smart and sustainable solutions."**
2. **"I master technical skills with passion and persistence."**
3. **"I think logically and creatively."**
4. **"My curiosity fuels my competence."**
5. **"I engineer not just systems, but change."**
6. **"I grow through experiments, errors, and excellence."**
7. **"Innovation flows through my mind and hands."**
8. **"My education equips me to uplift communities."**

9. **"I honour ethics and impact in every design."**
10. **"I am becoming a world-class engineer with heart."**

🌱 One Small Step

Tinker. Build. Break. Learn. Engineering begins with curiosity and grows through hands-on exploration. Choose one project, tool, or topic that excites you today. Dive in without fear. Every experiment is a step toward mastery. **Say softly:** ***"My vision builds. My passion leads. I am becoming."***

🙏 A Note to Close With

If you dream of building, solving, or innovating, trust that your future in engineering is already under construction. Every question you ask, every problem you try to solve, is a brick in your foundation.

"Engineers dream in logic and build in hope."

📓 Your Reflection Space

....

....

....

....

29. Manifesting Success as a Data Analyst or Data Scientist

"I decode stories in numbers and transform insight into action."

A Personal Insight

Data isn't just information; it's intelligence waiting to be unlocked. Becoming a data analyst or data scientist means more than working with numbers. It's about uncovering hidden patterns, telling stories through statistics, and guiding smarter, evidence-based decisions. Data is the language of progress, and those who learn to speak it fluently shape the future.

I was always fascinated by patterns, logic, and seeing the bigger picture. When I discovered data science, it felt like finding a bridge between curiosity and clarity, a discipline where exploration meets precision. It's a field where insights don't just stay in spreadsheets; they spark innovation, transform businesses, and solve real-world problems. Choosing this path is choosing to turn raw facts into powerful tools for change. *"I decode data. I discovered meaning. I lead through insight."*

🌈 A Moment to Visualise

Picture yourself diving into data, uncovering patterns others missed. With each dataset, you reveal answers that solve real problems, streamlining operations, improving lives, and guiding critical decisions. You're not just analysing numbers; you're activating intelligence. Every insight brings clarity, every chart reveals potential. You are empowered by the information at your fingertips, turning complexity into meaningful change. Through data, you're shaping the future, one discovery at a time.

Repeat gently… *"I turn data into direction. I transform complexity into clarity."*

✨ Today's Affirmations

1. **"I understand data with ease and curiosity."**
2. **"I turn raw information into actionable insights."**
3. **"I master tools and techniques with confidence."**
4. **"My mind is logical, focused, and evolving."**
5. **"I am a trusted problem-solver and strategic thinker."**
6. **"I decode patterns others don't see."**
7. **"I thrive in complexity and deliver clarity."**
8. **"My skills create value across sectors."**

9. **"I build ethical, intelligent solutions."**

10. **"I am becoming a data leader of tomorrow."**

🪶 One Small Step

Choose one dataset and pause to ask: "What story is this trying to tell?" Let curiosity guide your analysis. Use visualisation tools to reveal patterns, trends, and truths. Every graph is a window into insight. **Say softly: *"I turn data into stories. I see meaning in the details."***

🙏 A Note to Close With

Pick a dataset that intrigues you. Ask, "What story lives here?" Use charts, graphs, or maps to bring it to life. Let the data speak through your creativity and curiosity.

"Behind every number lies a need, a truth, a transformation."

📔 Your Reflection Space

....

....

....

....

30. Manifesting Success as a YouTuber

"I share my truth, inspire through my content, and connect with authenticity."

A Personal Insight

Being a YouTuber isn't about chasing views; it's about creating value. It's about turning your voice, your passion, and your unique perspective into something that educates, entertains, or empowers. YouTube is more than a platform; it's a powerful space where your creativity can reach hearts across the globe.

When I stepped into the digital world, I quickly realised that success isn't about going viral overnight. It's about being authentic, showing up consistently, and connecting with people in a meaningful way. It's about telling your story, sharing your skills, and being of service to your audience. The magic lies not in perfection, but in presence. Not in trends, but in truth.

A Moment to Visualise

Picture your YouTube channel filled with videos that reflect your passion, creativity, and voice. See yourself filming, editing, and uploading content that excites and fulfils you. Watch as your audience grows, connects, and engages, drawn not just to what you make, but to who you are. Feel the joy of being seen, heard, and valued for your authenticity. Every view, comment, and like becomes a reflection of your purpose.

Repeat gently… *"My content inspires, uplifts, and expands my reach."* So, *"I create with joy. I express with truth. I am enough, just as I am."*

✨ Today's Affirmations

1. **"I show up confidently in front of the camera."**
2. **"I create content that reflects my values."**
3. **"I connect deeply with my audience."**
4. **"My growth is aligned and organic."**
5. **"I am consistent and committed to my purpose."**
6. **"My creativity flows effortlessly."**
7. **"I am supported by a growing digital community."**
8. **"I receive feedback with openness and grace."**
9. **"My channel adds light to the internet."**
10. **"I am becoming a powerful voice in the digital world."**

🌿 One Small Step

Record a short video today about something you truly love, even if it's just for yourself. Don't worry about perfection. Let it be real, raw, and fully you. Every time you express yourself from the heart, you grow in confidence and clarity.

Say softly… ***"I honour my voice. I express with courage."***

🙏 A Note to Close With

You don't need fancy gear or a perfect setup. What truly matters is your unique voice, your light, your presence. Start where you are, with what you have. Let the world meet the real you, one honest, heartfelt video at a time.

"When your content comes from the soul, connection becomes inevitable."

📓 Your Reflection Space

…………………………………………………………………

…………………………………………………………………

…………………………………………………………………

…………………………………………………………………

31. Manifesting a Career as a Professional Lawyer

"I stand for truth, uphold justice, and advocate with courage."

A Personal Insight

Becoming a lawyer is not just about knowing statutes or citing cases; it's about standing for what is right. It's about being a voice for those who feel unheard, guiding people through complexity, and restoring faith in fairness. A legal career demands resilience, clarity, empathy, and the wisdom to speak with impact, not just volume.

When I imagined myself in this profession, I didn't first see a courtroom. I saw families finding hope, individuals finding direction, and justice being served not just through laws, but through integrity. To be a lawyer is to be a protector of truth, a defender of dignity, and a bridge between conflict and resolution. You are not just building a career; you are becoming a lighthouse for many in moments of uncertainty.

A Moment to Visualise

See yourself standing in a courtroom or sitting at a negotiation table. You speak calmly, clearly, and with conviction. Every word is measured, every pause intentional. You're not just arguing a point, you're representing truth with integrity. People listen, not because you demand attention, but because you've earned their respect. You are composed, trusted, and grounded in purpose. Your presence brings confidence, your voice brings justice.

Repeat softly… "My words serve justice. My strength supports those in need."

Today's Affirmations

1. **"I advocate with knowledge, fairness, and empathy."**
2. **"My mind is sharp, and my ethics are strong."**
3. **"I protect what's right with integrity."**
4. **"I learn and grow from every case and challenge."**
5. **"I uphold the law while honouring compassion."**
6. **"I am a voice of reason and resilience."**
7. **"My legal path aligns with purpose and service."**
8. **"I am trusted for my wisdom and dedication."**

9. **"I prepare with precision and perform with poise."**

10. **"Justice flows through the clarity of my words."**

🪶 One Small Step

Read one case study today in a field of law that inspires you, whether it's human rights, corporate law, or criminal justice. Take time to reflect not just on the outcome, but on how you would approach it. Let your values guide your reasoning and deepen your understanding.

Say softly: ***"I think with clarity. I act with purpose. I grow through reflection."***

🙏 A Note to Close With

Lawyers do more than win arguments; they help restore faith in justice and fairness. Every case you handle, every client you support, is a chance to build trust and make a difference. Walk your journey with deep responsibility and pride, knowing your work matters.

"When you speak for justice, the law walks beside you."

📓 Your Reflection Space

....

....

....

....

32. Manifesting Entry into Civil Services

"I prepare with focus, serve with pride, and rise with responsibility."

A Personal Insight

Civil service is more than just a profession; it is a profound commitment to serving the nation. It calls for not only excellence and endurance but also a deep sense of ethics. Above all, it requires individuals driven by the desire to bring about meaningful change.

When I envisioned myself in governance, I didn't focus on power or authority. Instead, I saw the opportunity to create purpose, where systems evolve, communities thrive, and a brighter future is shaped by strong values, clear vision, and integrity. Being part of the civil service means contributing to the common good and building a legacy of service, compassion, and leadership.

A Moment to Visualise

Imagine the moment you crack the civil service exam. Your name appears on the selection list, a realisation of your hard work and dedication. You walk into a training hall filled with passionate, future change makers. The air is charged with purpose.

You feel a deep sense of belonging, knowing that this is just the beginning of your journey to making a real difference in the world. You're ready to serve, lead, and create lasting impact.

Repeat softly… *"I serve with dignity. I prepare with discipline. I lead with heart."*

✨ Today's Affirmations

1. **"I study with unwavering focus and joy."**
2. **"My preparation aligns with divine timing."**
3. **"I retain knowledge easily and effectively."**
4. **"I am worthy of responsibility and trust."**
5. **"I am calm and confident in every interview and test."**
6. **"My dream to serve the nation is being realised."**
7. **"I believe in my purpose and potential."**
8. **"I carry my values into my service."**
9. **"The exam tests me, but it does not define me."**
10. **"I am becoming a proud officer of change."**

🌿 One Small Step

Set aside two uninterrupted hours today to focus on your toughest topic. Instead of feeling pressure, embrace the present moment. Dive deep into your studies with clarity and patience, allowing your mind to fully absorb the material. This dedicated time will bring you closer to mastering the subject.

🙏 A Note to Close With

You were not born to fit in; you were born to lead. Your purpose is to guide, inspire, and elevate others through your service. Embrace your unique path, knowing that your leadership has the power to make a difference. By uplifting others, you create a legacy of impact and change.

"Civil service is not about clearing an exam, it's about carrying a nation's hopes."

📓 Your Reflection Space

....

....

....

....

33. Manifesting a Life in Defence Services

"I embody discipline, valor, and the spirit of selfless service."

A Personal Insight

Defence is more than just a profession; it's a profound purpose. It is the quiet, unwavering courage that ensures every sunrise is met with peace. Choosing this path means dedicating yourself to protecting yourself without expecting applause, to lead without seeking recognition. When I envisioned wearing the uniform, I saw not just strength but also grace. I saw the sacrifices made to defend boundaries, and the deep bonds forged through honor and commitment.

Serving in the defence forces is not merely a job, but a calling one that demands integrity, sacrifice, and an unshakeable sense of duty. It is about serving your nation with your heart and soul, knowing that your actions contribute to the safety and security of countless lives. There is no higher honor than offering your life in service to your country.

A Moment to Visualize

Picture yourself in uniform, standing tall with pride and poise. As you salute the flag, you feel a deep sense of purpose, grounded in duty and honor. Your body is ready, your mind focused, and your mission clear. You serve not just because it's your responsibility, but from a place of deep inner devotion and commitment. Every action, every step you take reflects the pride of representing something greater than yourself, your country, your people, and the values you hold dear.

Repeat softly… *"I am strong, focused, and born to protect with pride."*

Today's Affirmations

1. **"I train my body, mind, and spirit to serve with honor."**
2. **"I am courageous in the face of fear."**
3. **"Discipline flows through my every action."**
4. **"I thrive under pressure and rise to challenges."**
5. **"My resilience defines me."**
6. **"I am destined for service and valor."**
7. **"I act with humility, courage, and clarity."**
8. **"I lead through action and integrity."**
9. **"My nation's safety is my sacred mission."**
10. **"I am becoming the soldier my country can trust."**

🙞 One Small Step

Wake early and challenge yourself, whether physically or mentally. Honor the discipline of the path you've chosen long before you wear the uniform. Every moment of effort strengthens your resolve, shaping you into the leader and protector you aspire to be. This commitment sets the foundation for your service ahead.

Say softly: ***"With every step, I grow stronger, focused, and ready to serve."***

🙏 A Note to Close With

Service isn't just about following orders; it resides in quiet resolve. It's in the commitment to stand tall, to protect what's sacred, and to serve with honor. You were born to carry this responsibility, not for recognition, but for the deeper purpose of safeguarding what matters most to others.

"When you walk for your country, every step becomes immortal."

📓 Your Reflection Space

....

....

....

....

34. Manifesting Success as a Physical Trainer or Health Expert Freelancer

"I transform lives through movement, mindset, and motivation."

A Personal Insight

Becoming a physical trainer or health expert is a sacred task, because you don't just shape bodies, you shape beliefs. You help people reclaim their power, discipline, and vitality, guiding them to rediscover their potential. It's more than physical transformation; it's about fostering mental resilience and emotional strength. I realized that the most powerful wellness coaches don't preach perfection, they walk with you through every step of progress.

They meet you where you are, encouraging growth and improvement, never judgment. They lead with empathy, empowering you to rise above challenges. Each rep, each word, and each habit build, not only physical strength but a mindset that embraces endurance and positivity. It's a journey of partnership, not just instruction, one that transforms lives, nurtures confidence, and elevates energy, turning struggles into triumphs, one step at a time.

🌈 A Moment to Visualize

See yourself guiding someone through a workout or nutrition session. Their face lights up with gratitude and newfound energy. You know you've helped them feel stronger, not just physically, but mentally. With every rep, every meal, you're not only shaping their body but empowering their confidence and belief in themselves.

Repeat softly: *"I inspire health. I radiate vitality. I lead others with heart."*

🌟 Today's Affirmations

1. **"I live in alignment with wellness and balance."**
2. **"I guide others through passion and knowledge."**
3. **"My clients trust my consistency and care."**
4. **"I grow stronger in my body, business, and purpose."**
5. **"Every workout is a doorway to inner transformation."**
6. **"I market my services with authenticity and value."**
7. **"I hold space for others to become their best."**
8. **"I am building a thriving, independent practice."**

9. **"My work creates ripples of health and hope."**
10. **"I am a leader in the wellness world."**

🌿 One Small Step

Share one tip, workout, or health insight with your audience today. It could be as simple as the importance of hydration, quick workout moves, or a mindful eating tip. Even a small message can spark change, motivating someone to take their first step toward better health and wellness.

Say softly: ***"With every word and action, I inspire transformation. My guidance helps others grow stronger, inside and out."***

🙏 A Note to Close With

You are the coach, the guide, and the light on someone's journey back to health. Your presence, energy, and commitment to their growth make all the difference. Show up in full power, knowing that every step you take leads them closer to strength and vitality.

"Your movement moves the world."

📓 Your Reflection Space

....

....

....

....

35. Manifesting the Vision of Owning a Showroom

"I open doors to abundance, beauty, and purpose-driven business."

A Personal Insight

Owning a showroom is more than just displaying products, it's about building a presence, creating an experience that resonates with your customers. It's about translating your vision into a space that reflects trust, style, and service. Whether it's fashion, furniture, cars, or art, your showroom becomes more than a retail space, it becomes your signature. Each item, each detail is carefully curated to tell a story and evoke an emotional connection with the visitors.

I imagined the shutters rising on something that was once just a dream in my journal. It's not just about selling; it's about creating an immersive experience, a place where customers feel inspired and understood. It's about offering more than products, it's about offering a lifestyle, an identity, a space where people can connect with the essence of what you represent. Through this, your showroom becomes a destination, not just a store.

A Moment to Visualise

Picture yourself unlocking your showroom for the day. As the lights come on, the space comes alive, with each display meticulously arranged, showcasing your products at their best. Clients step in, their eyes filled with admiration and interest.

The atmosphere hums with energy, a perfect blend of style and professionalism. You can feel the excitement in the air as people are drawn into your vision, ready to experience the quality, trust, and service you've worked so hard to create.

Repeat softly… *"I own a space that reflects my growth and offers value."*

Today's Affirmations

1. **"My showroom is a manifestation of excellence."**
2. **"I attract clients who value my offerings."**
3. **"Every detail of my space radiates abundance."**
4. **"I manage my business with clarity and grace."**
5. **"My products meet needs and desires beautifully."**
6. **"I lead with ethics and elevate my brand daily."**
7. **"Sales flow with ease and joy."**

8. **“My showroom tells my story through service.”**
9. **“I am proud of the empire I am building.”**
10. **“I am rooted in vision and rising in success.”**

🌿 One Small Step

Sketch or digitally design a layout for your dream showroom. Visualize every corner, display, and detail, and let your imagination guide you. See the space come alive in your mind before it becomes a reality.

Say softly: ***"I am designing my vision, and it is already coming to life."***

🙏 A Note to Close With

When you create something with heart, the world makes room for it. Your passion, vision, and dedication resonate, attracting the opportunities and people who will support it. Build it with unwavering belief, knowing that your authentic effort will pave the way for success and fulfilment.

“Your business is your canvas, paint it with passion.”

📓 Your Reflection Space

....

....

....

....

🙞 36. Manifesting a Journey as a Transformational Educator

"I light minds, shape hearts, and teach with love and truth."

A Personal Insight

Being an educator is not just about textbooks; it's about transformation. A teacher has the incredible ability to ignite lifelong confidence, curiosity, and courage in their students. The lessons shared can echo in a student's soul for decades, shaping their journey and empowering their potential. I knew I wanted to teach when I realised that knowledge is only truly powerful when shared.

Education is the gift that multiplies every time it's passed forward, impacting not only the student but their community and the world. Teaching is more than imparting facts; it's about inspiring minds to think critically, explore deeply, and dream beyond limitations. The impact of a great educator can transcend generations, creating a ripple effect that enriches lives and transforms futures. To teach is to give the gift of possibility, knowing that the power of knowledge will continue to grow and inspire long after it's shared.

A Moment to Visualise

See yourself standing before your students, young or old. Their eyes shine with understanding as they absorb the lessons you share. Your voice carries clarity, guiding them with care and purpose. You can feel the connection between you and them, knowing that your words are making a difference in their lives. The classroom becomes a space of growth, where curiosity is nurtured and confidence is built, one lesson at a time.

Repeat softly… *"I teach with clarity, compassion, and joy."*

Today's Affirmations

1. **"My classroom is a space of growth and trust."**
2. **"I adapt, evolve, and empower with each lesson."**
3. **"I teach to touch lives, not just deliver content."**
4. **"My knowledge flows with humility and hope."**
5. **"I am heard, respected, and remembered."**
6. **"I inspire both questions and answers."**
7. **"I nurture potential with patience."**
8. **"My teaching reflects my soul's service."**
9. **"I keep learning to keep teaching better."**
10. **"I am an educator who uplifts generations."**

One Small Step

Prepare a lesson plan or a short talk on a topic you love. Break it down into key points, ensuring it's engaging and informative. Teach it to one person or record it for yourself to review later. This exercise will help reinforce your understanding and improve your teaching skills.

Say softly: *"Every lesson I teach strengthens my knowledge and helps me grow as an educator."*

A Note to Close With

Educators plant seeds of knowledge that may never fully bloom, but the garden of growth continues to flourish, shaping minds and lives long after the classroom ends.

"Teaching is not what you do, it's who you become."

Your Reflection Space

....

....

....

....

37. Manifesting Harmony with My Boss and Professional Growth

"I grow in grace, not just position. I align with purpose, not just approval."

A Personal Insight

Workplaces are more than structures; they are ecosystems of energy, expectations, and exchange. Our relationship with a boss or leader often reflects more than just professional roles; it can mirror how we see authority, how we handle pressure, and how we define our own values. Sometimes this relationship flows smoothly. Sometimes it feels strained or misunderstood. Regardless of its form, we always have the power to choose how we show up with respect, clarity, and calm integrity.

True growth at work isn't just about promotions or praise. It's about alignment. When you operate from a place of confidence and purpose, your outer environment begins to shift. You no longer work for approval, you work in truth, and growth follows. Harmony with leadership doesn't mean surrender. It means setting boundaries with grace, communicating with presence, and trusting that you can thrive, even in complexity.

A Moment to Visualise

Close your eyes. Imagine your boss or direct superior standing before you. Notice any energy that arises: tension, respect, anxiety, neutrality. Simply witness it. Now, imagine a transparent bridge of light forming between you, built on calm communication, mutual respect, and shared growth. See tension dissolving, replaced by professionalism, clarity, and steady confidence in your own voice.

Repeat softly… *"I speak with calm, I work with integrity, I grow with ease."*

Today's Affirmations

1. **"I show up with professionalism, confidence, and grace."**
2. **"I maintain boundaries while staying open to collaboration."**
3. **"I am respected in my workplace because I respect myself first."**
4. **"My value is not determined by anyone else's opinion."**
5. **"I communicate with clarity and listen with intention."**
6. **"I align with growth that matches my purpose, not just my title."**
7. **"My energy shapes my work environment positively."**

8. **"I choose calm over reaction, and wisdom over ego."**

9. **"I am building bridges, not walls, in my career."**

10. **"I trust my journey to lead me to workplaces that nourish my growth."**

🌿 One Small Step

Today, write a short note or silently affirm gratitude for one skill or strength you've developed in your professional life, because of, or despite, your boss. Own it. Celebrate it. **Say softly:** ***"This is mine. I honour my evolution."***

🙏 A Note to Close With

Professional growth and personal growth are not separate paths. They often rise together. When you choose to work from a presence, to lead yourself first, and to remain rooted in self-worth, you manifest not just a better job, but a better version of yourself in that space.

"I don't just work, I evolve. And I attract roles, mentors, and paths aligned with my truth."

📔 Your Reflection Space

....

....

....

....

38. Manifesting the Life of an Actor or Musician

"My voice, my expression, my story is meant to be seen and heard."

A Personal Insight

The stage isn't just a platform; it's a reflection of the soul, a space where your inner truth can be shared with the world. Becoming an actor or musician isn't about chasing fame or recognition; it's about telling authentic stories, evoking emotions, and creating connections that resonate deeply with others. When you align your passion with discipline and stop waiting for permission to shine, that's when you truly step into your light. Creativity flourishes where courage and consistency meet.

It's the quiet commitment to showing up, practising your craft, and staying true to your art that turns dreams into reality. Embrace the journey, trust in your ability, and watch as your unique gifts unfold. It's in this dedication that true artistry is born full of heart, soul, and endless possibility.

A Moment to Visualise

See yourself on stage or in the studio, eyes closed, heart open, and your voice flowing effortlessly. Feel the energy of the space, the resonance of your performance, and the warmth of applause. Let the moment fill you with fulfilment and joy, knowing that your art is alive and making a lasting impact. Let go and let your creativity flow freely.

Repeat softly… *"I am a creative force. I express my soul with fearless joy."*

Today's Affirmations

1. **"I own the stage of my life."**
2. **"My talent is unique; my voice is needed."**
3. **"Every day I grow in skill and confidence."**
4. **"My passion finds its way to the right people."**
5. **"I am consistent in nurturing my craft."**
6. **"I express emotion with power and grace."**
7. **"I am worthy of being seen, heard, and celebrated."**
8. **"My journey is unfolding perfectly."**
9. **"I make space for inspiration and discipline."**
10. **"I am already the artist I dream of becoming."**

🌿 One Small Step

Record a short performance even if only for yourself. Watch it, feel it, and celebrate it. You showed up. ***Say softly: "I am proud of this moment, of my courage, and the art I've shared. Every step forward is a victory."***

🙏 A Note to Close With

You don't need to wait for discovery. Discover yourself first. Create, share, and shine again and again. Your unique light is meant to be shared with the world, and every step you take brings you closer to your true potential.

"Your voice is not noise, it is legacy."

📔 Your Reflection Space

....

....

....

....

39. Manifesting the Power to Write a Book

"My words matter. My voice is ready to shape the world."

A Personal Insight

Writing a book isn't reserved for experts, celebrities, or scholars; it's for anyone who has a story, a message, or a truth yearning to be shared. If you feel that inner nudge to write, then you are already a writer. The most important step is to trust your voice and the unique perspective only you can offer.

Yes, the process can be intimidating, with blank pages, self-doubt, and fear of what others might think. But when you write from your heart, you create something honest and powerful. Each word becomes a step toward healing for yourself and for those who will one day read your words. Let your writing be an act of love, not pressure. You're not here to impress, you're here to express. Your story matters, and someone out there needs to hear it. Begin.

A Moment to Visualise

Close your eyes and envision your name shining boldly on the cover of a beautifully bound book. Feel the warmth of pride as you turn each page, filled with your words, your truth, and your unique voice.

Picture readers across the world, holding your book close, finding comfort, inspiration, and healing within your story. Some may cry, others may smile, but all will feel something real. Your words carry power, your story holds meaning, and only you can bring it to life. The world is ready to begin.

Repeat softly: *"I am ready to share my truth. My words are powerful and needed."*

Today's Affirmations

1. **"My voice matters. My story is valuable."**
2. **"Each word I write brings me closer to completion."**
3. **"I am a channel of inspiration and truth."**
4. **"My writing helps others and heals me."**
5. **"I let go of perfection and allow flow."**
6. **"My book is already written in spirit, I am now bringing it to life."**
7. **"I am disciplined, inspired, and creative."**
8. **"I show up to write even when it's hard."**

9. **“I trust my message will reach those who need it.”**

10. **“I am an author. I am ready.”**

🪶 One Small Step

Open a fresh page and begin to write just one paragraph. Not for approval, not for perfection, but for you. Let your thoughts spill without judgment, without filter. Let it be honest, raw, and completely your own.

Say aloud: ***"My words flow freely. I express myself with honesty, courage, and heart."***

🙏 A Note to Close With

Your words will land exactly where they’re meant to touch the hearts and minds that need to hear them. The book you dream of writing is already within you, patiently waiting to unfold. Start today, even with just one sentence. Trust in your voice, your message, and remember your story matters.

“I don’t wait for the perfect time; I create it word by word.”

📔 Your Reflection Space

....

....

....

....

40. Agile Project Management in Corporate Enterprises

"Leadership in projects isn't about control; it's about guidance and empowerment."

A Personal Insight

As a project manager in corporate environments, your role goes beyond simply overseeing timelines and budgets. It's about leading teams, navigating challenges, and ensuring that every project aligns with the broader company goals. Project management requires a balance of skill, empathy, and foresight, understanding both the micro details and the macro-objectives. The best project managers don't just manage, they inspire, empower, and guide teams through every obstacle with clarity and purpose.

In any project, the most important asset is the people you work with. Your leadership is crucial in creating a collaborative environment where every team member feels valued and motivated to achieve a common vision. Your decisions set the tone for success, and when you choose to lead with trust and empathy, the outcomes will naturally follow.

A Moment to Visualise

Imagine yourself leading a successful project with a dedicated team. The team collaborates seamlessly, working toward the same goal. Your communication is clear, and your guidance fosters confidence and alignment. Picture the satisfaction of delivering a project on time, within budget, and above expectations, knowing that your leadership made it possible.

Repeat softly… *"I lead with clarity, compassion, and purpose, bringing success to every project."*

Today's Affirmations

1. **"I lead with clarity, guiding my team toward successful project outcomes."**
2. **"Every challenge is an opportunity for growth and innovation in my projects."**
3. **"I foster collaboration and open communication within my project teams."**
4. **"My strategic planning ensures projects are completed on time and within budget."**
5. **"I inspire confidence and motivation in my team members."**
6. **"I adapt to changes with resilience and a positive mindset."**
7. **"I manage resources efficiently, maximising productivity and quality."**
8. **"I build strong relationships with stakeholders, ensuring alignment and support."**

9. **"I celebrate milestones and achievements, recognising the efforts of my team."**
10. **"I continuously seek opportunities to improve and refine project management processes."**

🌱 One Small Step

Reach out to one team member today, offering feedback or appreciation. Strengthen your connection with your team and create an environment where they feel empowered and supported in achieving their best work.

Say aloud: "I actively connect with my team, offering feedback and appreciation to foster an environment where everyone feels empowered and supported in achieving their best work."

🙏 A Note to Close With

Being a project manager is more than just managing; it's about leading with heart and purpose. Reflect today on the qualities that make you a great leader and write down one way you can improve in your current project.

"Leadership is not about being in charge; it's about taking care of those in your charge."

📓 Your Reflection Space

....

....

....

....

41. Strategic Human Resources: Shaping Corporate Success

"HR is not about hiring; it's about building the culture that sustains the future."

A Personal Insight

Human Resources is the backbone of any organisation. It's about aligning the company's vision with the talent it nurtures. HR professionals are the custodians of company culture, helping create an environment where employees thrive. By fostering collaboration, resolving conflicts, and ensuring clear communication, HR enables the organisation to build a unified team focused on common goals. HR is not about filling vacancies; it's about creating a thriving ecosystem where everyone can contribute, grow, and succeed.

A successful HR strategy is built on understanding people, their needs, and their aspirations. When you approach HR with empathy, respect, and fairness, you build a workforce that's not only skilled but also motivated and aligned with the organisation's core values. Your role as an HR manager is to guide, nurture, and empower, creating a workplace that attracts and retains the best talent.

A Moment to Visualise

Close your eyes and imagine a harmonious workplace where everyone feels valued. Employees work collaboratively, supporting each other, and the organisation's goals are in perfect alignment with their personal values. Picture yourself in an HR meeting, discussing a new initiative to enhance employee well-being, and feel the positive impact you are creating.

Repeat softly… *"I foster a workplace that nurtures growth, respect, and collaboration."*

Today's Affirmations

1. **"I create a work environment where everyone feels valued and heard."**
2. **"I foster collaboration, respect, and inclusivity within my organisation."**
3. **"I attract top talent that aligns with the company's mission."**
4. **"I manage employee relations with empathy, understanding, and care."**
5. **"I empower teams by nurturing their potential and growth."**
6. **"My HR decisions are rooted in fairness, respect, and integrity."**
7. **"I lead with compassion, ensuring a supportive and healthy workplace."**

8. **"I am a catalyst for positive change in the workplace."**
9. **"I foster a culture of open communication and mutual respect."**
10. **"I guide my organisation toward becoming a magnet for talent and innovation."**

🌱 One Small Step

Connect with one employee today, ask how they're doing, and listen to their thoughts. Make them feel heard and appreciated, strengthening your role in creating a supportive workplace environment.

Say aloud: ***"I actively engage with my team, offering feedback and appreciation to foster a positive and empowering workplace."***

🙏 A Note to Close With

HR management is about people first. Take a moment to reflect on how you contribute to your organisation's culture. Write down one action you can take to enhance employee satisfaction and well-being.

"The best way to predict the future is to create it, starting with the people around you."

📔 Your Reflection Space

....

....

....

....

Limitless Wealth and Prosperity

42. Manifesting Abundant Wealth through Investment Planning

"My investments are seeds of abundance. I nurture them with wisdom and watch prosperity bloom."

A Personal Insight

True wealth is not built overnight; it is the patient art of tending to what matters most. Investment planning is more than financial charts or market trends; it's about envisioning a future where your dreams are safely held and steadily nurtured. Every plan you make, every goal you set, every wise choice you act upon is a silent promise to your future self: *I am preparing for your freedom.* Wealth is not about chasing quick wins. It's about creating sustainable peace, empowerment, and joy. When you invest wisely, time, energy, and money, you are saying "yes" to a future of independence and ease. You are trusting the process of slow, beautiful growth.

A Moment to Visualise

Find a quiet space. Take a few deep breaths. Now, imagine holding a small, glowing coin in your hands. This coin holds your dreams, your security, your hopes.

Visualise yourself planting it in rich, fertile soil. Watch as, over time, it sprouts strong trees bearing fruits of opportunity, comfort, and freedom. Feel a deep trust in your heart: you have started a journey toward abundance that will never stop giving back.

Repeat softly… *"I plant wisely. I wait patiently. I receive abundantly."*

✵ Today's Affirmations

1. **"I attract opportunities that align with my vision of financial freedom."**
2. **"Each investment decision strengthens the foundation of my abundant future."**
3. **"I nurture a mind-set of patience, wisdom, and steady growth."**
4. **"My financial choices align with my long-term dreams and values."**
5. **"I trust my intuition and research to guide me toward prosperous outcomes."**
6. **"Every resource I invest multiplies with purpose and clarity."**
7. **"I create a financial life rooted in security, freedom, and joy."**
8. **"My investment journey reflects my dedication to abundance and mindful living."**
9. **"I celebrate each small win as a sign of growing prosperity."**

10. **"I am a powerful creator of lasting wealth and opportunity."**

🌿 One Small Step

Take a moment today to review one area of your financial life, whether it's savings, investments, or budgeting. Visualise yourself making small, steady adjustments that build a strong, abundant foundation for the future you desire and deserve.

Say aloud: ***"Each wise step I take today creates a future of freedom and abundance."***

🙏 A Note to Close With

Investment planning is not about chasing fast gains; it's about building a legacy of confidence, peace, and prosperity. Reflect on how every intentional choice you make today nurtures a future where your dreams are not just imagined but fully lived.

"Wealth is not built in a moment; it is nurtured with every wise choice, every patient step, and every dream fiercely believed in."

📓 Your Reflection Space

....

....

....

....

43. Manifesting Target Sales with Alignment and Ease

"I serve with purpose, I sell with honesty, and I grow with grace."

A Personal Insight

Sales isn't about pressure, persuasion, or pushing people to say yes; it's about creating genuine connections. When you truly believe in what you offer and stand behind the value it brings, success becomes a natural result of that alignment. Set ambitious goals, absolutely, but let them be grounded in service, not scarcity. When your energy flows from joy, clarity, and purpose, it attracts the right clients, the right conversations, and sustainable income.

You don't have to chase; just show up with heart. Offer value, build trust, and stay open. People feel sincerity. Let your sales process reflect who you are, not just what you're selling. Detach from the outcome. Anchor your actions in authenticity, and the right results will come, not through force, but through resonance. That's where lasting growth and meaningful impact begin.

A Moment to Visualise

Close your eyes and visualise your monthly sales target being met with ease. Orders are flowing in steadily; clients are not just satisfied, they're genuinely grateful for your service. You feel aligned, focused, and empowered. But your happiness doesn't come solely from hitting the numbers.

It stems from the meaningful connections you're building, the value you're delivering, and the difference you're making. This success feels fulfilling because it reflects purpose, not just performance. You're thriving, and it's well deserved.

Repeat softly… *"I attract aligned clients. I achieve my goals with ease."*

Today's Affirmations

1. **"I trust the value of what I offer."**
2. **"My sales are a reflection of the joy I bring."**
3. **"I release pressure and focus on connection."**
4. **"Clients find me easily and are excited to work with me."**
5. **"I sell with authenticity, not fear."**
6. **"I meet my targets with flow and faith."**
7. **"Money flows to me through joyful service."**
8. **"Every sale is a blessing to both me and the buyer."**

9. **"I celebrate every milestone, big or small."**
10. **"I am aligned, abundant, and achieving with ease."**

🌿 One Small Step

Reach out to one potential client or lead today, not with pressure to sell, but with a genuine intent to help. Share insight, offer value, and build trust. Let authentic connection guide the way.

Say aloud: ***"I lead with authenticity, offer with heart, and build connections rooted in trust."***

🙏 A Note to Close With

You're not chasing sales; you're sharing meaningful solutions. Approach each opportunity with purpose, not pressure. Trust the value you offer, your energy, and your expertise. When your intention is rooted in service, success flows naturally. The right clients will come, and the numbers will follow.

"My goals are not a burden; they are proof of what's possible."

📓 Your Reflection Space

....

....

....

....

44. Manifesting Money with Gratitude and Flow

"I am a magnet for financial abundance. Money flows to me with ease and purpose."

A Personal Insight

Money is not just a currency; it's a reflection of energy, mindset, and flow. When you view it through the lens of fear, stress, or scarcity, it feels distant and hard to hold. But when you welcome it with trust, gratitude, and an open heart, it begins to move with ease. True abundance doesn't start with your bank account; it begins with your beliefs.

You are already rich in creativity, kindness, and potential. When you focus on the value you bring to others, when you serve with joy and remain open to receiving, money naturally follows. Let today be the day you shift your relationship with money. Release the fear, the shame, the old stories. Make space for financial peace, purpose, and freedom rooted in alignment and faith. Abundance is not a chase, it's a choice.

A Moment to Visualise

Close your eyes. Picture yourself receiving money with ease and joy through your talents, your inspired ideas, your aligned work, and even through unexpected blessings. You feel safe, supported, and abundant. You smile as you give generously, invest wisely, and grow with confidence. Money becomes a tool of freedom, not stress. It flows in and out of your life like a calm, steady breath, natural, rhythmic, and always enough. You no longer fear money; you trust it. You no longer chase it; you attract it. Let this vision anchor you in peace and possibility. You are worthy of overflow. You are ready to receive.

Repeat Softly… *"I receive money with gratitude. I use it with wisdom and joy. I am aligned with wealth, and abundance flows to me with ease."*

Today's Affirmations

1. **"I welcome money into my life with ease."**
2. **"Abundance surrounds me and flows to me freely."**
3. **"I am open to new streams of income."**
4. **"I release scarcity and choose trust."**
5. **"I attract wealth through purpose and joy."**
6. **"Money supports my dreams and values."**
7. **"I am financially free, stable, and secure."**
8. **"I am worthy of receiving and keeping abundance."**

9. **"I bless every dollar/rupee I spend and receive."**
10. **"Money flows to me in miraculous ways."**

🌱 One Small Step

Take a moment to list five ways money has already appeared in your life, whether through a paycheck, a gift, a discount, a refund, or unexpected support. Big or small, it all counts. Acknowledge each one with gratitude and say aloud: ***"Thank you, Universe. I welcome more joy. More, please."***

🙏 A Note to Close With

You are not asking for too much; you are simply remembering your worth and claiming what has always been possible for you. Your desires are not excessive; they are expressions of your inner truth. The energy you send through your intentions, actions, and beliefs is already finding its way back to you. Trust that your dreams are valid, and your timing is divine. Stay open, stay grounded, and know that what you seek is already seeking you in return.

"Wealth begins in the mind, flows through intention, and returns through trust."

📓 Your Reflection Space

....

....

....

....

45. Manifesting the Millionaire Mindset

"I am aligned with abundance, and I attract wealth with purpose and peace."

A Personal Insight

Becoming a millionaire begins in the mind. It starts when you shift your perspective on money, not as a struggle or something to be feared, but as a stream of energy. Money flows naturally to those who create, serve, and align with value, not through force or desperation.

When I transitioned from a mindset of scarcity to one of possibility, everything around me began to change. I stopped chasing after money and started creating opportunities. I realised that abundance is not something to chase, it's a channel. It's an energy that flows when you align with it, when you take intentional actions, and when you believe that it's already on its way to you. Opening that channel requires clarity, consistent effort, and trust in your ability to receive. The more you align your thoughts and actions, the more abundance flows effortlessly into your life.

A Moment to Visualise

Close your eyes and visualise your bank account growing steadily. See wealth flowing effortlessly from your aligned actions, honest intentions, and creative pursuits. Picture yourself managing this abundance with confidence, gratitude, and generosity, using it as a tool to enrich your life and positively impact those around you.

Repeat gently… *"Money flows to me as I serve and grow. I am ready to receive."*

Today's Affirmations

1. **"I welcome wealth with wisdom and responsibility."**
2. **"Money flows through me to do good in the world."**
3. **"I am building lasting financial freedom."**
4. **"I think like a millionaire, I plan, I act, I believe."**
5. **"Abundance is my natural state."**
6. **"I use money as a tool to empower and uplift."**
7. **"I trust my ability to create sustainable wealth."**
8. **"My mindset is magnetic to opportunities."**

9. **"I celebrate the success of others and attract my own."**
10. **"I am financially free and spiritually grounded."**

🌿 One Small Step

Track your income and spending today consciously. Treat money like a sacred tool, not just a number. Use it with intention and respect, knowing it is a resource that supports your dreams.

Say softly: ***"I honour the flow of money and use it wisely."***

🙏 A Note to Close With

Millionaires aren't made overnight because they're shaped through consistent daily choices, a bold vision, and unwavering persistence. Each step, no matter how small, contributes to building lasting success and wealth. Stay focused, stay committed, and trust the process.

"You're not chasing millions. You're becoming the person millions align with."

📔 Your Reflection Space

....

....

....

....

46. Manifesting Financial Assistance with Dignity

"I am supported by the universe in every form, seen and unseen."

A Personal Insight

Asking for financial help can often feel like admitting defeat, but it is one of the most powerful acts of faith and courage. I've learned that receiving is not a sign of weakness; it is simply part of the natural cycle of giving. We are not meant to walk alone in lack. Sometimes, abundance flows to us through others. When we seek assistance with openness, humility, and intention, we invite grace into our lives.

The right help will always find you when you are aligned with a sense of worthiness and clarity, not when you're coming from a place of desperation. It's about trusting that help is part of the flow, and that by allowing others to support you, you are contributing to the greater cycle of giving and receiving that keeps the world in balance.

A Moment to Visualise

Picture yourself receiving a call, message, or meeting where someone offers you exactly what you need, whether it's funds, advice, or opportunities. Feel open and your breath deepen as you receive this gift. In that moment, say thank you from your soul, fully embracing the abundance that flows to you.

Repeat softly… *"It's safe to receive. I am worthy of help and support."*

Today's Affirmations

1. **"The universe meets my needs through kind, timely hands."**
2. **"I ask for what I need without shame."**
3. **"Help flows to me from aligned and abundant sources."**
4. **"Financial support uplifts my path and strengthens my purpose."**
5. **"I am open to receiving, always with gratitude."**
6. **"I trust the divine timing of provision."**
7. **"Money comes to me through known and unknown channels."**
8. **"I am surrounded by generous, helpful people."**
9. **"Each step I take invites financial flow."**
10. **"Receiving is part of abundance."**

🪶 One Small Step

Write down one person, institution, or grant you could reach out to. Take that step today with clarity and confidence, knowing that your action is aligned with your goals and purpose. Every small move brings you closer to your vision.

Say softly: ***"I am taking aligned action today, reaching out with confidence and clarity. Every step brings me closer to my goals, and I trust the process."***

🙏 A Note to Close With

You are not alone. Help is not just a hand, it's a divine bridge, guiding you from where you are to where you're meant to go. Embrace the support that comes your way, knowing it's part of your journey to growth and fulfilment.

"Asking opens doors. Receiving opens hearts."

📓 Your Reflection Space

....

....

....

....

Health and Fitness

47. Manifesting Successful Surgery with Courage & Calm

"My body is in safe hands. I trust the process and surrender to healing."

A Personal Insight

Facing surgery can be one of life's most tender and vulnerable experiences. It can stir up fear, uncertainty, and a sense of losing control. But within that vulnerability lies the powerful potential for healing, renewal, and transformation. While the mind may race, the spirit can still find stillness, and when you calm your spirit, your body listens and responds with greater ease.

Surgery is not only a medical process, but also a sacred collaboration between science, skilled hands, and the deep wisdom of your body. Trust in your doctors, trust in your body's resilience, and trust in your own strength. You are not walking through this alone. Every breath, every heartbeat, is part of your healing. Let your body know: you are safe, you are supported, and you are moving through this with unwavering faith and grace.

A Moment to Visualise

Close your eyes and envision yourself being gently prepared for surgery. The medical team around you is calm, kind, and skilled, ensuring an atmosphere of safety and trust. You feel completely relaxed. The procedure unfolds effortlessly, each step carried out with care and precision. When you awaken, there is light and peace surrounding you, and you feel comforted. Your healing process begins, steady and sure, as your body embraces the strength and grace it holds.

Repeat softly… *"I am safe. I am strong. I trust my healing path."*

Today's Affirmations

1. **"My surgery is guided by skilled, compassionate hands."**
2. **"I am calm, grounded, and protected."**
3. **"I trust my body to respond beautifully to care."**
4. **"Healing begins the moment I choose peace."**
5. **"I am surrounded by support, seen and unseen."**
6. **"I release fear and welcome a smooth recovery."**
7. **"My body knows how to heal and regenerate."**
8. **"Each breath carries strength into every cell."**

9. **"I trust life's timing and the wisdom of this decision."**

10. **"This experience is part of my greater healing journey."**

🌿 One Small Step

Place your hand gently over your heart and say aloud**: *"I am safe. I am whole. I am ready to heal."*** Feel the warmth of your hand, allowing those words to sink deeply into your body. Let that sense of calm and assurance settle, bringing peace and readiness to heal.

🙏 A Note to Close With

You are not alone in this journey. Every step of your healing is embraced by divine care, surrounded by love and support. Trust that each moment brings you closer to renewal. Let courage be your guide, lifting you, while faith wraps around your heart, providing comfort, strength, and unwavering peace. You are supported, seen, and cherished. Each breath you take is a reminder that you are never walking this path by yourself. Healing is already happening, and you are safe in this process.

"My body heals because my soul believes."

📔 Your Reflection Space

....

....

....

....

48. Post-Treatment Recovery for Heart, Brain, Liver, and Vital Organs

"Every breath, every beat, every moment is a step back to my strength."

A Personal Insight

Recovering after medical treatment, particularly when it involves vital organs like the heart, brain, or liver, is not only a physical process but also a journey that touches your emotions and spirit. Your body has experienced something profound, and now it needs patience, stillness, and an abundance of love to heal fully. This is a time to trust in your body's wisdom, to release any lingering fear, and to allow your body to do what it was naturally designed to do to heal. You are not broken.

You are in the process of rebuilding. You are not weak; you are becoming stronger with each passing moment. Every breath you take, every moment of rest, every positive thought you have, is essential medicine for your recovery. Trust that your body knows what it needs and honour the space it requires to restore itself. Healing is already unfolding.

A Moment to Visualise

Close your eyes. Imagine your organ, your heart, your brain, your liver glowing with soft light. Visualise blood flowing, renewing cells, tissues strengthening. Let this inner light radiate wellness.

Repeat softly… *"I am healing. I am whole. I honour the wisdom within my body."*

Today's Affirmations

1. **"My recovery is unfolding perfectly in its own time."**
2. **"I listen to my body's needs and honour its signals."**
3. **"My heart beats stronger each day."**
4. **"My mind is clear, peaceful, and focused."**
5. **"My liver renews and restores with ease."**
6. **"My organs are aligned, supported, and healing beautifully."**
7. **"I am patient with the process."**
8. **"Rest is my responsibility and my strength."**
9. **"I give my body permission to receive complete healing."**
10. **"I am a living miracle in motion."**

🌿 One Small Step

Close your eyes and gently place your hand over the organ you're healing. Feel the warmth of your touch, and softly whisper: ***"You are safe. I believe in your strength. You are capable of healing, and I trust in your body's ability to restore itself."*** Let these words bring comfort and peace.

🙏 A Note to Close With

Recovery is a sacred journey of renewal. Let love be your medicine and rest your greatest healer. Your body, mind, and spirit are aligning to return to wholeness. You are coming back not just physically, but fully, embracing every part of your being in the healing process.

"I return to myself stronger, wiser, and more alive than ever before."

📔 Your Reflection Space

....

....

....

....

49. Manifesting Recovery from Critical Illness

"My spirit is unbreakable. My healing is inevitable."

A Personal Insight

When faced with a critical illness, it's easy to feel overwhelmed, frightened, or isolated. The journey can feel long, uncertain, and full of challenges. But even in the darkest hour, the light of your spirit never fades. Healing doesn't always follow a straight path; it rises slowly, deeply, and steadily. Every step you take, no matter how small, is a step toward restoration. You are not defined by your diagnosis; you are so much more.

Your body is resilient, your soul is fierce, and your energy is an unyielding force. With the right care, mindset, and support, recovery doesn't just become possible; it becomes inevitable. Trust that your body knows what it needs and has the strength to heal. Every moment of hope you nurture within is a medicine far more powerful than you realise. Keep believing in your healing.

A Moment to Visualise

Close your eyes and imagine yourself surrounded by a golden, warm, healing light. It wraps around you, protective and soothing, gently touching every part of your body. Feel the light penetrate deep within, comforting and revitalising. With each breath, you grow calmer and stronger. Your body responds, embracing the healing energy. Trust in this moment. You are not just resting, you are actively healing, regaining strength, and nurturing your body with each passing second.

Repeat softly… *"I am recovering with grace. My body knows what to do."*

Today's Affirmations

1. **"I am not defined by illness; I am defined by strength."**
2. **"My body is healing in ways I cannot yet see."**
3. **"I am surrounded by love, support, and divine care."**
4. **"My recovery is unfolding in perfect timing."**
5. **"I honor what my body has survived."**
6. **"Every breath brings renewal and relief."**
7. **"My thoughts support my healing."**
8. **"I am allowed to rest and be held."**
9. **"I trust the process, even in uncertainty."**
10. **"Healing flows through every cell of my being."**

🙞 One Small Step

Place both hands gently on your heart and say: ***"You've carried me this far. I trust you to take me further. I honour your strength, your wisdom, and your resilience. Together, we will continue this journey, moving forward with trust and love."***

🙏 A Note to Close With

Even when your body feels weak, your soul remains unshakable. Trust in the strength that resides within you. Each moment, no matter how small, is a step toward healing and wholeness. Allow yourself the grace to heal at your own pace, with unwavering faith.

"I rise from this with a deeper love for life and a stronger love for myself."

📔 Your Reflection Space

....

....

....

....

50. Manifesting Recovery from Diabetes

"Balance flows through me. I live in harmony with my body's rhythm."

A Personal Insight

Living with diabetes is a journey that requires awareness, responsibility, and self-care. However, it doesn't have to be a path defined by fear. With each mindful choice, whether it's about diet, exercise, or managing stress \ you move closer to balance, strength, and vitality. Diabetes doesn't strip you of your power; rather, it awakens it. It teaches you to listen more closely to your body, to understand its signals, and to honour its needs every single day.

True healing and progress aren't measured by numbers alone; they come from nurturing yourself holistically. You can thrive despite the challenges. Every step you take toward caring for your health, both physically and emotionally, strengthens you. You are resilient, and your journey is one of growth, empowerment, and continual healing. Embrace your strength and know that you have the power to flourish.

🌈 A Moment to Visualise

Imagine your body functioning with perfect balance. Your blood sugar remains stable, your energy is high, and every cell is in harmony, working together effortlessly. You feel light, strong, and capable.

Your mind is clear, your body is resilient, and you are in complete control. Every system is working optimally, and you are thriving, not just surviving. This is the natural state of your being: vibrant, healthy, and full of vitality.

Repeat softly… *"I honour my health. I create balance with every breath."*

🌟 Today's Affirmations

1. **"I manage my health with wisdom and grace."**
2. **"I nourish my body with care and compassion."**
3. **"My lifestyle choices support healing."**
4. **"My pancreas is functioning with ease."**
5. **"I maintain balance effortlessly."**
6. **"I release fear and welcome control."**
7. **"Each day, I grow healthier and stronger."**
8. **"I love and respect my body's needs."**
9. **"Healing is always happening inside me."**
10. **"I am empowered in my healing journey."**

🌿 One Small Step

As you eat your next meal, take a moment to pause and say: ***"This food is my fuel. This moment is my medicine."*** Let each bite nourish your body, mind, and spirit, knowing that you are supporting your health with intention and care.

🙏 A Note to Close With

You are not at war with your body; you are working in harmony with it. Trust the process, even when it feels slow. Celebrate every small victory and progress along the way. Your body is resilient, and with patience and care, you are doing beautifully. Keep honouring yourself, each step matters.

"I walk in harmony with my healing, one step at a time."

📔 Your Reflection Space

....

....

....

....

51. Manifesting a Healthy Heart

"Every beat of my heart is strong, steady, and sacred."

A Personal Insight

Your heart is more than just a muscle; it is the rhythm of your life, the pulse that carries your emotions and experiences. It is the silent partner in every breath you take, working tirelessly to keep you alive. Caring for your heart goes beyond physical health; it means nourishing your mind, body, and soul with love, balance, and compassion. Even when it is strained or under stress, your heart is doing its best.

With each beat, it communicates with you, sending signals for movement, nourishment, and peace. Listen closely and honour its needs. Your love for yourself is the most powerful medicine your heart responds to. Treat yourself with kindness, patience, and rest, and watch your heart return to its natural state of vitality. When you show love to yourself, your heart finds strength to heal.

A Moment to Visualise

Close your eyes and imagine your heart surrounded by a soft, pulsating glow. With every breath you take, feel the glow grow stronger, filling your heart with warmth and peace. Each beat is steady and calm, supported by the love and care you give to yourself.

This healing light surrounds your heart, nourishing it with comfort and resilience. Trust in your body's natural ability to heal, knowing your heart is growing stronger and more peaceful with every passing moment.

Repeat softly… *"I am grateful for my heart. I nourish it with love and calm."*

Today's Affirmations

1. **"My heart beats in harmony with my body."**
2. **"I care for my cardiovascular health with intention."**
3. **"I choose peace over pressure."**
4. **"Each heartbeat is a gift I cherish."**
5. **"I move gently and breathe deeply for my heart's health."**
6. **"I release stress and welcome serenity."**
7. **"My heart is healing and growing stronger every day."**
8. **"I listen to my body's wisdom."**

9. **"I make choices that honour my heart."**

10. **"Love flows to and from me freely."**

🌿 One Small Step

Place your hand gently over your heart and take three slow, calming breaths. As you breathe, say softly: ***"Thank you for every beat. I am here with you."*** Feel the connection between you and your heart, honouring its rhythm and supporting its strength.

🙏 A Note to Close With

Your heart is loyal, beating tirelessly for you, even when it's weary. Now, it's your turn to show up for it. Nourish it with love, care, and patience. Honour its resilience and offer it the rest and peace it so deeply deserves.

"In honouring my heart, I deepen my connection to life itself."

📔 Your Reflection Space

....

....

....

....

52. Manifesting Glowing Skin

"My skin reflects the harmony within me."

A Personal Insight

Radiant skin is a sign of inner alignment. I used to chase perfect products, thinking beauty could be bottled. But as I slowed down, drank more water, ate intuitively, and spoke kindly to myself, I saw my glow return naturally. Beautiful skin is not just about serums; it's about softening your self-talk. It's a reflection of your peace, your nourishment, and your ability to let go of stress.

When I started listening to my body with love and treating my daily rituals as self-care instead of punishment, everything changed. I realised that your skin isn't just your outer layer, it's your story. And it deserves to be nurtured with the same devotion you show to your dreams. Even in moments of breakouts or dullness, I reminded myself: healing is happening. Self-kindness, consistency, and deep nourishment became my skincare routine.

🌈 A Moment to Visualise

Close your eyes and imagine your reflection bathed in soft, natural light. Run your fingers gently across your cheeks, feeling the smoothness, warmth, and ease of your skin. You smile not because of how others see you, but because of how you feel in your own skin. With each breath, you walk into your day with radiance and grace, knowing that your true glow comes from within. Your inner light shines through, effortlessly radiating beauty, confidence, and peace.

Repeat softly… *"My light shines from within, and I move through the world with grace, confidence, and peace."*

✨ Today's Affirmations

1. **"My skin heals with every loving thought I think."**
2. **"I nourish myself from the inside out."**
3. **"I radiate natural beauty and confidence."**
4. **"I am gentle with my self-image."**
5. **"I trust my body to glow in its own time."**
6. **"My glow comes from peace and presence."**
7. **"I choose rituals that replenish and restore."**
8. **"I love my skin and the story it tells."**
9. **"I am radiant, luminous, and divine."**
10. **"My outer glow reflects my inner harmony."**

🌿 One Small Step

Drink a full glass of water with gratitude, feeling it nourishes your body. As you apply your skincare, do so with mindfulness, honouring the ritual. Let each step be a moment of self-care, kindness, and appreciation for the body you're nurturing.

Say softly: ***"I hydrate with gratitude, nourish with intention, and honour my body with every mindful step."***

🙏 A Note to Close With

Your glow is the reflection of your inner truth. Treat it with love, honour, and gentleness. It is a beautiful expression of who you are, radiating from within, so care for it with kindness and reverence.

"When your heart is light, your skin follows."

📔 Your Reflection Space

....

....

....

....

53. Manifesting Confidence in Growing Taller

"I rise with grace, stretch with strength, and grow in self-belief."

A Personal Insight

Growing taller isn't just about inches, it's about standing taller in your own truth. Often, when we feel small inside, we carry that feeling in our posture. We hunch, we shrink, as if trying not to be noticed. But when we begin to believe in our growth, whether physical, emotional, or spiritual, our body naturally aligns with that belief. I remember, as a child, I would hunch, trying to make myself smaller, less visible.

But when I started affirming my own worth and consciously working on my posture, everything changed. I stood taller, breathed more deeply, and radiated newfound confidence. The shift wasn't just physical; it was internal. Sometimes, the height we're truly seeking isn't measured by inches; it's the height of self-worth, confidence, and presence. When we believe in our values, our body responds, and we stand in truth, unapologetically.

🌈 A Moment to Visualise

Visualise yourself growing a little taller each morning. Feel your spine gently elongating, your shoulders relaxing and straightening, and your chin lifting with newfound confidence. With every breath you take, your body becomes more aligned, standing taller and stronger.

See yourself walking through your day with presence, strength, and grace, radiating self-assurance with each step. Your posture reflects the belief you hold in yourself, and you move with the quiet power that comes from truly embracing who you are. Every movement embodies your growth inside and out.

Repeat gently… *"I rise in strength. I stretch into my full potential."*

✨ Today's Affirmations

1. **"I feel tall, confident, and grounded in my body."**
2. **"My posture improves as I honour my presence."**
3. **"Growth is my natural state."**
4. **"I nourish myself with positive beliefs."**
5. **"I release tension and stand with pride."**
6. **"I love how tall and strong I feel each day."**
7. **"Stretching and self-care support my growth."**

8. **"My body aligns with the energy of upward movement."**
9. **"I accept and enhance my unique form."**
10. **"I rise, physically and mentally."**

One Small Step

Stand in front of a mirror, roll your shoulders back, take a deep breath, and say aloud: ***"I honour my growth."*** Feel the strength in your posture and the power in your words, acknowledging how far you've come and the growth within you.

A Note to Close With

Whether your goal is physical or emotional height, stand tall in your own story. Embrace your journey with confidence, knowing that growth comes when you believe in your rightful place in the world. Own your space, and let your growth unfold from within.

"The tallest you'll ever be is when you stand in your truth."

Your Reflection Space

....

....

....

....

54. Manifesting Healthy, Regular Periods

"I welcome my body's natural rhythm with care and compassion."

A Personal Insight

Your menstrual cycle is not a burden; it's a natural rhythm, a symbol of vitality, flow, and inner harmony. While irregular periods may bring uncertainty, discomfort, or even shame, remember this: your body is not failing you. It's communicating, asking you to slow down, listen, and support it with care. Healing isn't just about dieting or rest; it starts with how you speak to yourself. Harsh self-talk creates tension; gentle words invite restoration. Offer your body compassion. Treat it as an ally, not an obstacle.

Trust your womb, it holds ancient wisdom and listens deeply. When you nurture it with patience and respect, it begins to feel safe, and balance follows. You are not broken; you are beautifully alive, cycling through nature's flow. Honour your body, and it will respond with grace and strength.

A Moment to Visualise

Close your eyes. Imagine your body as a blooming garden, vibrant, fertile, and full of life. Each breath nourishes it, each moment grounds it. See a steady, gentle river flowing through this sacred space, symbolising your natural cycle, fluid, rhythmic, and in perfect harmony with nature. Feel the calm in that flow, steady and sure.

This is your body's wisdom in motion. The garden doesn't rush to bloom, nor does the river force its way; it all unfolds with grace. Trust in your rhythm, in your body's quiet intelligence. You are not out of sync; you are simply learning to listen. Let this vision remind you of your strength and softness coexisting beautifully. You are whole, and your cycle is not a disruption; it's a divine, life-giving flow waiting to be honoured.

Repeat softly… *"I welcome balance. I trust my body to find its rhythm."*

Today's Affirmations

1. **"I trust my body to regulate with time and care."**
2. **"I release stress and make space for balance."**
3. **"My cycle is a reflection of my inner harmony."**
4. **"I nourish myself with rest and rhythm."**
5. **"My body is wise and capable of healing."**
6. **"I celebrate my femininity without fear."**

7. **"Every day, my hormones align with love."**
8. **"I am patient and kind to myself through the process."**
9. **"I am not broken, I am blooming."**
10. **"My womb is a space of life, not shame."**

🌿 One Small Step

Place a warm, gentle hand over your lower abdomen and softly say: ***"Thank you, body. I trust you. I love you."*** Breathe into that space. Feel the warmth, the connection, and the quiet reassurance growing stronger with each breath. Let your body know it's safe, seen, and supported.

🙏 A Note to Close With

You are not behind or broken. Your body is simply learning to feel safe in the space you create. Be patient with its pace. Be gentle with your thoughts. Healing takes time, and you're doing beautifully.

"My body speaks to me in cycles. I am learning to listen to them."

📓 Your Reflection Space

....

....

....

....

55. Manifesting Long, Healthy Hair

"My hair grows with love, strength, and self-care."

A Personal Insight

Hair is not just a feature; it's a symbol of vitality, nourishment, and care. Often, we look at the mirror and judge what we see, forgetting that hair, like all of us, needs patience and love.

Healthy hair begins from within. It's in the thoughts we think, the nutrients we take in, and the rest we offer ourselves. By shifting your focus from frustration to faith, you allow your hair to flourish under care, not criticism.

You are not losing hair; you're shedding old energy. Let what grows next be nourished by your new mindset.

A Moment to Visualise

Imagine running your fingers through soft, strong strands of your own hair, thick, shiny, and full of life. Each strand feels healthy, vibrant, and cared for. You see it flowing with natural strength, reflecting the love and patience you've poured into yourself.

You smile, not out of vanity, but pride. Because you know this isn't just about hair, it's about the way you've shown up for your well-being, one nourishing choice at a time. And it shows.

Repeat softly… *"I care for my hair with love. It grows beautifully and abundantly."*

✨ Today's Affirmations

1. **"My hair is a reflection of my inner nourishment."**
2. **"Each strand grows with care, strength, and vitality."**
3. **"I release the fear of hair loss and invite regrowth."**
4. **"I feed my body with nutrients and my mind with peace."**
5. **"I love my hair at every stage."**
6. **"Patience and care bring healthy growth."**
7. **"My scalp is healthy; my roots are strong."**
8. **"I bless my hair with love and intention."**
9. **"I radiate confidence in my natural beauty."**
10. **"My hair flourishes under my loving care."**

🌿 One Small Step

Massage your scalp gently today using warm oil or just your fingertips. As you do, speak with love: ***"I nourish you. I believe in your growth."*** Let each stroke be a gesture of care, inviting strength, renewal, and deep trust in your body's natural rhythm.

🙏 A Note to Close With

Like every living thing, your hair thrives with love, gentle care, and consistent attention. Trust the process, even when growth feels slow. Every strand, every inch is a sign of progress. Celebrate what's blooming; it's a reflection of your patience, your nurturing, and your quiet strength.

"What I water with kindness, flourishes."

📓 Your Reflection Space

....

....

....

....

56. Manifesting Pregnancy with Trust and Love

"My body is ready. My womb is sacred. I am open to new life."

A Personal Insight

The pregnancy journey is deeply emotional. At times, it's filled with hope, at others, with uncertainty. But within you lies the power to nurture, to carry, and to welcome life.

You are not behind. You are not broken. Your body is listening. It needs your love, not your pressure. When you soften into trust and honour your sacred femininity, you begin to align with the rhythm of creation itself. Let each day be an invitation, not an expectation. Let love guide you, not fear.

A Moment to Visualise

Close your eyes and envision a warm, golden light gently flowing through your womb. It glows softly, bringing peace, calm, and comfort to this sacred space. Feel its warmth nourishing every cell.

This is a place of creation, safety, and love. Imagine a new life beginning to form here quietly, naturally, and beautifully aligned with you.

Repeat softly… *"I trust my body. I trust the timing. I welcome life."*

✵ Today's Affirmations

1. **"I am worthy of motherhood."**
2. **"My womb is ready, soft, and sacred."**
3. **"I nourish my body with care and love."**
4. **"I release fear and embrace faith."**
5. **"I trust the process, even when I cannot see it."**
6. **"I welcome this journey with an open heart."**
7. **"My body knows how to conceive and carry."**
8. **"Each moment is preparing me to receive life."**
9. **"I am in alignment with my highest fertility."**
10. **"New life is on its way to me."**

One Small Step

Place your hands gently over your womb and whisper softly, ***"You are safe. You are scared. You are loved."*** Let the vibration of these words sink deep into your body. Feel the warmth rising beneath your palms, a tender promise of care and connection. This space holds strength, softness, and infinite wisdom. Honour it fully.

🙏 A Note to Close With

You are co-creating with life itself, a sacred dance between your body, your spirit, and the universe. Be gentle with your heart, especially in moments of uncertainty. Trust your body's wisdom and timing, even when it's quiet. Let love be the guide, the force that moves you forward with grace, patience, and unwavering faith.

"I bloom with trust, I rest in hope, and I wait with love."

📓 Your Reflection Space

....

....

....

....

57. Manifesting Freedom from Drug Addiction

"Each day I choose clarity over chaos, healing over habit."

A Personal Insight

You're not starting over, you're starting stronger, with experience, courage, and clarity. The path you've walked has already shown your strength. The hardest part, deciding to change, is behind you. Now, every breath you take, every moment you choose wellness over old patterns, is a quiet act of self-respect. You are no longer surviving, you're reclaiming. You're choosing life with every step, even when it's tough.

You are not broken; you are rebuilding, wiser and more aware. Remember, healing isn't linear, and progress isn't perfect. Keep choosing breath. Keep choosing presence. Keep choosing for yourself. Because each time you say no to what once controlled you, you say yes to the life waiting to unfold with clarity, freedom, and strength.

🌈 A Moment to Visualise

Close your eyes and visualise yourself standing tall, shoulders relaxed, breathing in deeply. Your heart is calm, your mind clear. You feel grounded, empowered, and completely free.

This is not a moment of shame; it's a moment of strength. You've chosen healing, and that is a sacred, powerful act. Each breath affirms your progress, your courage, and your unwavering commitment to yourself. In this space, you are whole, worthy, and moving forward with grace and intention.

Repeat softly: *"I am healing. I am growing. I am free."*

✨ Today's Affirmations

1. **"I am not my past, I am my progress."**
2. **"Each craving I overcome makes me stronger."**
3. **"I deserve to feel whole and alive."**
4. **"My future is bigger than this habit."**
5. **"I breathe through discomfort and choose calm."**
6. **"I honor my body by protecting my peace."**
7. **"I forgive myself and focus on healing."**
8. **"Every day I stay clean is a day of victory."**
9. **"I have the power to change my story."**
10. **"Freedom begins with each conscious breath."**

🌱 One Small Step

Each morning, stand before the mirror, meet your own eyes, and say with conviction: ***"I am proud of who I'm becoming."*** Let this simple affirmation plant seeds of confidence and self-love. Over time, it becomes more than just words; it becomes your truth, your identity, and your guiding force through each day.

🙏 A Note to Close With

Addiction may have once spoken loudly, demanding your attention and shaping your choices, but your voice, the one rooted in healing, hope, and strength, is growing stronger each day. With every mindful breath, you are gently reclaiming control and coming back to who you truly are.

This journey isn't about erasing the past but embracing your power to begin again. Each moment of awareness brings you closer to freedom, clarity, and the version of yourself you've always deserved to be.

"I rise from the ashes of my pain; whole, worthy, and ready for more."

📔 Your Reflection Space

....

....

....

....

58. Letting Go of a Toxic Relationship

"I release what dims my light and make room for peace."

A Personal Insight

Not every relationship is meant to last forever. Some come into your life to teach, some to reflect who you are, and others to reveal what you no longer need. Letting go of a toxic connection is not an act of cruelty; it's a powerful stand for your own well-being. Toxic relationships deplete your spirit, confuse your truth, and pull you away from your path. Choosing to walk away is not a sign of weakness but of strength and self-awareness. It means choosing peace over chaos, clarity over confusion, and healing over harm.

You're not turning your back on love; you're turning toward self-respect. You're not abandoning someone; you're finally choosing not to abandon yourself. This is how you return to your own energy, your balance, and the freedom you've always deserved.

A Moment to Visualise

Close your eyes and gently suggest someone whose presence no longer supports your growth or peace. See them slowly and softly fading into the distance, like a wave returning to the sea. Notice how your body begins to release the weight you've carried, your shoulders feel lighter, your chest expands, and your heart feels freer. With every breath, you reclaim your space, your calm, and your emotional clarity. You are not losing, you're creating room for healing and truth.

Repeat softly… *"I release you. I return to me."*

Today's Affirmations

1. **"I trust myself to let go of what hurts."**
2. **"My peace is worth protecting."**
3. **"I deserve love that uplifts, not drains."**
4. **"I am no longer available for chaos."**
5. **"I walk away from pain with dignity."**
6. **"I choose boundaries over guilt."**
7. **"I forgive and release, not for them, but for me."**
8. **"The ending is not failure, it's freedom."**
9. **"My space is sacred, and I honour it."**
10. **"I choose love that begins with me."**

🪶 One Small Step

Write a heartfelt letter to the person or pattern you're choosing to let go. Pour your emotions onto the page, no filters, no holding back. You don't need to send it. Instead, tear it or burn it safely. As the paper fades, let your spirit feel lighter, freer, and ready to move forward.

Say aloud: ***"I release what no longer serves me, and I open my heart to new beginnings."***

🙏 A Note to Close With

Letting go is not a sign of loss, it's a powerful return to yourself. It's the moment you choose clarity over confusion, self-worth over struggle, and inner peace over chaos. In releasing what no longer serves you, you create space for joy, healing, and freedom. Let peace walk beside you as your constant, calming companion.

"When I choose peace, I make no apology for the boundaries I build."

📔 Your Reflection Space

....

....

....

....

59. Letting go of a Loved One who has Passed Away

"Though their presence is gone, their love lives on within me."

A Personal Insight

Loss creates a space within us where no one else can occupy, a silent presence that lingers in familiar places and cherished memories. When someone we love passes on, their absence shows up in unexpected moments: a song, a scent, an old photograph. Grief is not linear. It ebbs and flows, surprising us with its depth one day and its gentleness the next. It doesn't demand closure; it asks for compassion. Letting go doesn't mean forgetting; it means making room for joy again, while still holding their memory with tenderness.

Love doesn't disappear when someone leaves this world. It transforms into stories we tell, lessons we carry, and the warmth we feel when we think of them. In continuing to live fully, we honour them. Their presence becomes a quiet strength that walks beside us, always.

A Moment to Visualise

Close your eyes and gently picture your loved one smiling at you. Feel their warmth wrapping around you like a quiet embrace, their energy steady and comforting. Let that love fill the space around you, soft yet strong. Now, place your hand over your heart, the place where their memory lives, not in sadness, but in gratitude. They are with you, always, in every breath and every beat.

Repeat softly… *"I miss you. I love you. I live on, carrying your light."*

Today's Affirmations

1. **"I allow myself to grieve and to grow."**
2. **"Their love still guides me."**
3. **"It's okay to feel joy again."**
4. **"I honour their memory by living fully."**
5. **"I am never truly alone."**
6. **"I speak to them in quiet moments, and I feel heard."**
7. **"I carry their wisdom in my heart."**
8. **"My tears are part of healing, not weakness."**
9. **"I release guilt and embrace peace."**
10. **"Love endures, even in absence."**

🌾 One Small Step

Light a candle or write a heartfelt letter to your loved one. Recall a cherished memory, speak the words you've been holding inside. Let your emotions flow freely onto the page or into the flame. As the candle burns, imagine its glow carrying your love, your thoughts, and your peace across time and space.

Say aloud: ***"I carry your love in my heart, always and forever."***

🙏 A Note to Close With

You carry their legacy in the way you live each day, with kindness, resilience, and purpose. It shows how you love others, how you rise after hardship, and how you keep moving forward. Let their love guide your steps and be the strength behind your every breath.

"They may be gone from sight, but never from your soul."

📓 Your Reflection Space

....

....

....

....

Miscellaneous

60. Manifesting a Greener Planet through Plantation

"Each seed I sow is a promise to the Earth and a prayer for generations."

A Personal Insight

Planting trees is one of the most beautiful and profound ways to give back to the Earth. In a world that is often overwhelmed by speed, technology, and constant motion, grounding ourselves in the soil offers a quiet, healing reprieve. A tree doesn't just grow; it nurtures the environment around it. It provides shade, purifies the air, and offers shelter and sustenance.

Every time I plant something, I feel as though I'm entering a silent but meaningful dialogue with nature itself. The earth receives what we give it in stillness, and in time, it responds with life. When we plant with intention, we are not merely growing trees; we are cultivating peace, nurturing life, and creating a legacy. Each tree we plant is a testament to our commitment to the planet and future generations.

A Moment to Visualise

Visualise yourself holding a small sapling, feeling the cool, damp soil in your hands as the warmth of the sun kisses your face. Gently dig a hole, place the roots with care, and cover them softly. Water the sapling with love and intention.

Watch it grow tall over time, thriving because of the nurturing energy you've given it. Each moment of care is a step toward life, and this tiny plant stands as a reminder of your ability to nurture and grow.

Repeat softly… *"I grow with the Earth. I give it back to the world. I plant hope."*

Today's Affirmations

1. **"With each tree I plant, I nurture future generations."**
2. **"I am connected to nature's cycle of growth and balance."**
3. **"My hands heal the earth, and the earth heals me."**
4. **"Every plant I sow multiplies life, oxygen, and beauty."**
5. **"I am a guardian of green and a student of silence."**
6. **"Planting gives me purpose beyond today."**
7. **"Even a single seed can spark a forest."**

8. **"I honour my responsibility to protect the planet."**

9. **"Nature blooms where my compassion meets action."**

10. **"I am proud to be part of Earth's renewal."**

🌿 One Small Step

Visualise yourself holding a small sapling, feeling the damp soil in your hands and the warmth of the sun on your face. Gently dig, place the roots, and cover them with care. Water it with love, knowing this tiny plant will grow tall because of you.

Say softly: ***"With every act of care, growth unfolds."***

🙏 A Note to Close With

The planet doesn't ask for everything, just a little care, a little action, and a little hope. Each tree you plant is a prayer, each act of nurturing a promise to the Earth. In these small gestures, you contribute to a better, greener world.

"When you plant a tree, you plant yourself in tomorrow."

📓 Your Reflection Space

....

....

....

....

61. Manifesting a Smooth Visa Approval

"Doors open for me with grace. I move across borders with ease and purpose."

A Personal Insight

Waiting for a visa can often feel filled with uncertainty, as if your plans are on hold, waiting for a simple stamp to move forward. But I've learned to replace worry with readiness. A visa is not just a stamp on a piece of paper; it's an affirmation from the universe that your journey is meant to continue beyond where you are. It represents trust in your path and the opportunities waiting for you.

When I let go of fear and instead focused on preparation with positivity, the process felt less like a stroke of luck and more like alignment. I realised that every step, every document, and every moment of patience was part of creating space for my next chapter. Approval didn't feel like a stroke of luck; it felt like everything was falling into place, just as it was meant to.

A Moment to Visualise

See yourself receiving that long-awaited visa; your passport now carries a golden stamp of possibility. Feel the surge of joy, the wave of relief, and the promise of new beginnings.

Visualise the open sky calling your name, your bags being packed with purpose and dreams. Imagine each folded outfit as a step toward freedom. You're smiling, heart brimming with excitement. This moment is yours, alive with anticipation, guided by trust, and blessed by the universe's perfect timing.

Repeat softly… *"I am ready, I am welcome, and I am moving forward."*

Today's Affirmations

1. **"Every document I submit is blessed with clarity."**
2. **"My intentions are pure and supported."**
3. **"The visa process works in my favour."**
4. **"I visualise my journey unfolding smoothly."**
5. **"I attract timely approvals and aligned travel."**
6. **"I move toward my purpose with preparation and patience."**
7. **"Immigration officers see my truth and value."**

8. **"My heart travels before my body does."**
9. **"I claim the right to move, grow, and explore."**
10. **"I travel not to escape, but to expand."**

🪶 One Small Step

Prepare one aspect of your application, or practice calm breathing when thinking about your interview. Take a few moments to visualise yourself speaking with ease and confidence. Review a key strength or achievement that you're proud of. Organise your documents, check your outfit, or rehearse your opening lines. Let your breath slow and deepen, inhale peace, exhale pressure. Trust that each step you take is guiding you closer to your goal.

Say aloud: ***"I am ready. I am calm. I will shine."***

🙏 A Note to Close With

Visas may be issued by authorities, but permission to journey begins within. Approve yourself first, and the world follows. When you believe in your worth, the universe aligns in quiet ways. You become magnetic to opportunities, open doors, and green lights. Start by validating your dreams, honouring your path, and walking forward with certainty. The moment you say yes to yourself, life echoes back with a louder yes. *"I am already approved by the universe within me."*

"When you carry clarity, every border becomes a bridge."

Your Reflection Space

....

....

....

....

62. Manifesting a Dream Holiday

"I deserve rest, joy, and beauty in my life, and I call it in with ease."

A Personal Insight

A dream holiday isn't just about a destination; it's about feeling alive again. It's about pausing, refreshing, and remembering that we are meant to experience pleasure and peace. When I allowed myself to plan joyfully, not guiltily, the universe aligned the way. You don't have to wait for the 'right time', you create it. Your dream escape begins with permission to feel free.

Let your soul breathe. Picture yourself waking up to the sound of waves, sipping something warm, barefoot and unhurried. Feel the sunlight kiss your skin, the breeze reminding you how natural it is to feel light and happy. Joy doesn't need permission from anyone but you.

Say softly: ***"I permit myself to rest, to explore, to feel good. I deserve moments that heal and lift me."***

A Moment to Visualise

Visualise the beach, mountain, city, or village of your dreams. The fresh sea breeze smells of crisp mountain air or aromatic street food. Taste the flavours that awaken your senses. Feel the warmth of sunlight on your skin or the crunch of snow beneath your feet. Let your body soften, your breath deepen, your heart smile. This moment is yours, real in sensation, alive in spirit.

Repeat softly… *"This joy is mine. This moment is real. I received my dream getaway."*

✵ Today's Affirmations

1. **"I allow myself the gift of rest and travel."**
2. **"I attract resources, plans, and support for my trip."**
3. **"My dream destination is already reaching me."**
4. **"I visualise myself fully present, peaceful, and happy."**
5. **"Travel opens my heart and soul."**
6. **"Joy and rest are not luxuries; they're necessary."**
7. **"I honour my desires and celebrate my life."**
8. **"I make space for fun and exploration."**
9. **"I trust the timing and direction of my travels."**
10. **"My soul knows where it wants to go, and I listen."**

One Small Step

Create a vision board or journal entry for your dream trip. Let it be vivid, heartfelt, and intentional. This is not just planning, it's manifesting.

Where: A serene cottage by the Amalfi Coast, Italy, where lemon trees bloom and time slows down.

When: Spring of next year, when the air is warm but gentle, and the flowers are in full bloom.

How: With savings set aside, flight booked with excitement, and an open heart ready to receive. I'll stay in a cosy B&B, explore local markets, and walk by the sea every morning.

Why: Because I crave stillness, beauty, and reconnection with myself, with joy, and with the magic of new places. This trip is a thank you to my soul for holding on through every storm.

Say aloud: ***"I trust the journey, and I welcome the beauty and magic life has in store for me."***

A Note to Close With

Your life was never meant to be lived only in duty. It was also meant to be lived in wonder in moments that light you up, in places that make your soul dance, in pauses that feel like poetry.

"Sometimes the journey your soul needs is to remember it can breathe."

Your Reflection Space

....

....

....

....

🙏 Final Gratitude Message to You, Dear Reader

As you turn these final pages, I want to pause and thank you for showing up, for believing in healing, and for choosing to hope when it wasn't always easy. This journey was never just about the words written here; it was about you reclaiming your own light. Every affirmation you whispered, every reflection you penned, became a seed of transformation, quietly blooming toward the life you were always meant to live.

May this journal continue to be your quiet companion in moments of growth and your faithful mirror, reflecting the truth of who you are beneath all the noise: radiant, resilient, powerful beyond measure.

Thank you for walking this path with me. Your presence has not only fulfilled a vision but has breathed life into a dream. With all my heart, all my soul, and all my gratitude**, Shilpy Tandon**

Final Affirmations Collection

A collection of affirmations to return to, any day, any time.

- **For Grounding:**
  - "I am safe, rooted, and supported."
  - "In this moment, I have all I need."
- **For Confidence:**
  - "I believe in my power and trust my path."
  - "I am aligned with my highest potential."
- **For Healing:**
  - "I am allowed to rest, reset, and rise again."
  - "Each breath is a step toward peace."
- **For Abundance:**
  - "I am a magnet for prosperity and possibility."
  - "I open my arms wide to receive all good things."

❖ **For Love:**

- "I am deeply loved and deeply loving."
- "I attract relationships that reflect my worth."